Leckie × Leckie
Scotland's leading educational publishers

Active LEA

Curriculum for Excellence

Fourth Level

BUSINESS & ENTERPRISE

Norma Mathieson

CONTENTS

CONTENTS

MARKETING A BUSINESS

BUSINESS OPERATIONS

BUSINESS FINANCE

BUSINESS REACHING THE CUSTOMER

HOW TO USE THIS BOOK

Leckie & Leckie's Active Learning series has been developed specifically to provide teachers, students and parents with the ability to implement Curriculum for Excellence as effectively as possible. Each book has been written with the following objectives in mind:

- To support the implementation of Curriculum for Excellence in schools.
- To engage students by taking a contextualised learning approach and providing a range of rich task activities.
- To assist teachers with the planning and delivery of lessons and assessment.

COVERING CURRICULUM FOR EXCELLENCE

Active Business and Enterprise comprehensively covers the Fourth Level Outcomes and Experiences for *Business and Enterprise*.

The Outcomes and Experiences have been organised into chapters, with a different topic covered on each double page spread.

The key topic knowledge is enhanced by a practical example, illustration or case-study to reinforce learning. A *Top Tip* is also included to highlight key information.

ADDRESSING THE PRIORITIES OF CURRICULUM FOR EXCELLENCE

Active Business and Enterprise Fourth Level focuses on methods to implement the philosophy underpinning Curriculum for Excellence. It addresses Curriculum for Excellence in a thoroughly practical way that makes learning both engaging and fun!

- Ideas for rich task activities are provided for every topic to enable pupils to gain experiences as well as learning outcomes.
- Paired and group learning activities encourage students to take responsibility for and direct their own learning, while developing the four capacities.
- Creative ideas are offered for making cross-disciplinary links with other classroom subjects, within the Social Studies faculty and, more widely, to help ensure students join-up their learning.
- The relevance of each topic to everyday life is highlighted in order to help students transfer their skills and knowledge to other areas of their lives.

The toolkit of ideas, subject links and activities contained in *Business and Enterprise* can be used in the classroom and/or at home. Please see pages 5–7 for details of the text design and key features of the book.

Each double page spread includes the following features:

ACTIVITIES page. This page contains questions and rich tasks to deepen understanding of each topic.

MAKE THE LINK box. This box highlights the relevance of the topic to a number of other school subjects. This enables learners to gain a more holistic understanding of each topic.

DID YOU KNOW? box. This box contains an additional fact about each topic to engage further interest and to bring the subject to life. It can also be used as an extension activity to broaden and deepen learning.

OUR EVERYDAY LIVES box. This box provides an example of how each topic relates to real life, in order to demonstrate its practical relevance.

END OF UNIT FEATURES

After each topic, *Active Business and Enterprise* has the following features that encourage deeper exploration of the topic and provide the means for self- and peer-assessment:

INTERDISCIPLINARY PROJECT Rich task activities around each unit to bring learning to life; ideas for interdisciplinary project work.

ACTIVITIES Further activity-based tasks, for individual, paired, or group exploration.

A learning checklist to help students assess and improve their own progress.

KEY FEATURES

Each double page spread contains the following features (see below). In addition, after each spread, there are even more activities as well as tools to help track progress.

KEY WORDS
Most important words and phrases highlighted in bold

EXAMPLES
Examples given are captivating and spark students' interest

FULL COLOUR
Bright and stimulating colour throughout

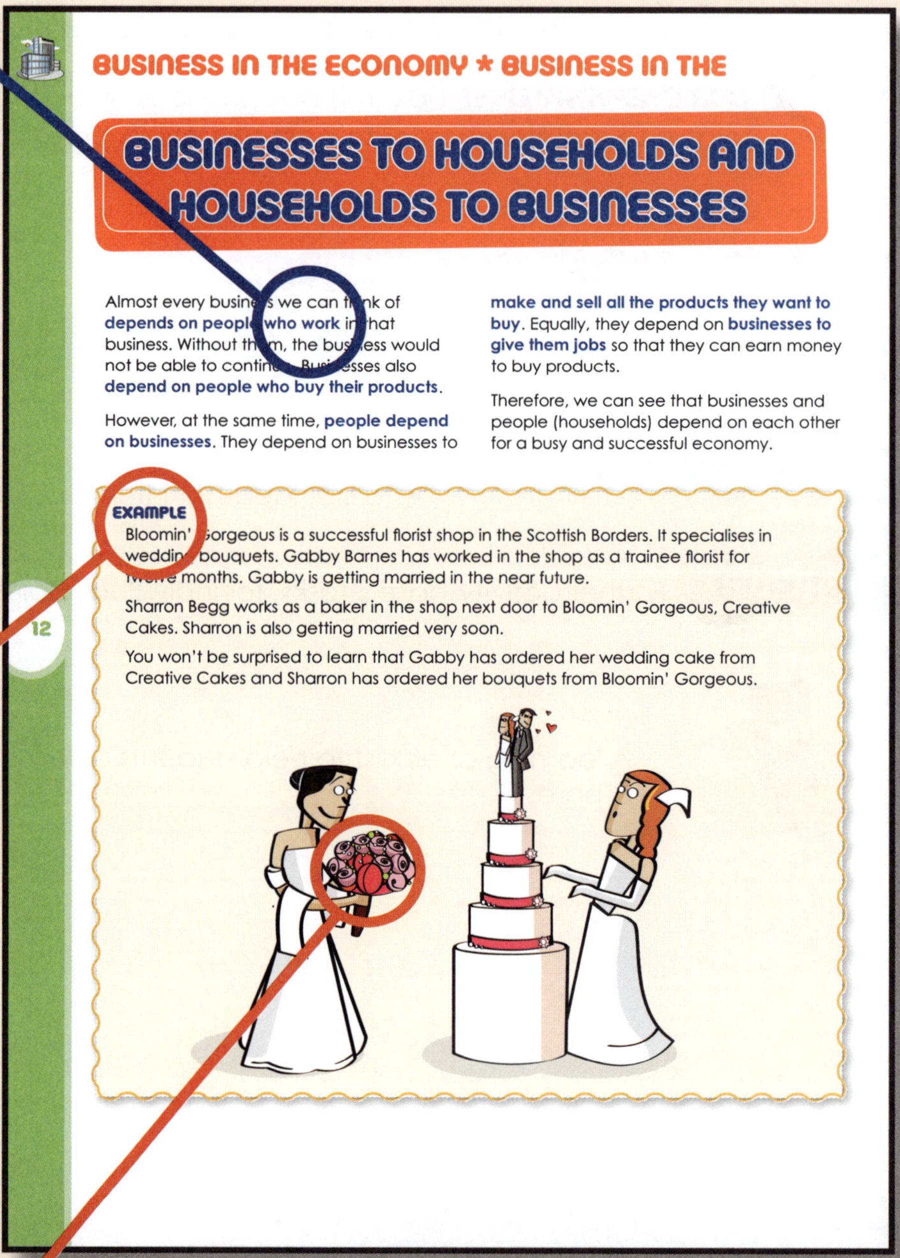

BUSINESS IN THE ECONOMY * BUSINESS IN THE

BUSINESSES TO HOUSEHOLDS AND HOUSEHOLDS TO BUSINESSES

Almost every business we can think of **depends on people who work** in that business. Without them, the business would not be able to continue. Businesses also **depend on people who buy their products**.

However, at the same time, **people depend on businesses**. They depend on businesses to **make and sell all the products they want to buy**. Equally, they depend on **businesses to give them jobs** so that they can earn money to buy products.

Therefore, we can see that businesses and people (households) depend on each other for a busy and successful economy.

EXAMPLE

Bloomin' Gorgeous is a successful florist shop in the Scottish Borders. It specialises in wedding bouquets. Gabby Barnes has worked in the shop as a trainee florist for twelve months. Gabby is getting married in the near future.

Sharron Begg works as a baker in the shop next door to Bloomin' Gorgeous, Creative Cakes. Sharron is also getting married very soon.

You won't be surprised to learn that Gabby has ordered her wedding cake from Creative Cakes and Sharron has ordered her bouquets from Bloomin' Gorgeous.

12

ACTIVITES TO TRY
Short and engaging revision questions and rich tasks

MAKE THE LINK
draws out links between subjects on a particular topic to aid Interdisciplinary learning and deepen understanding

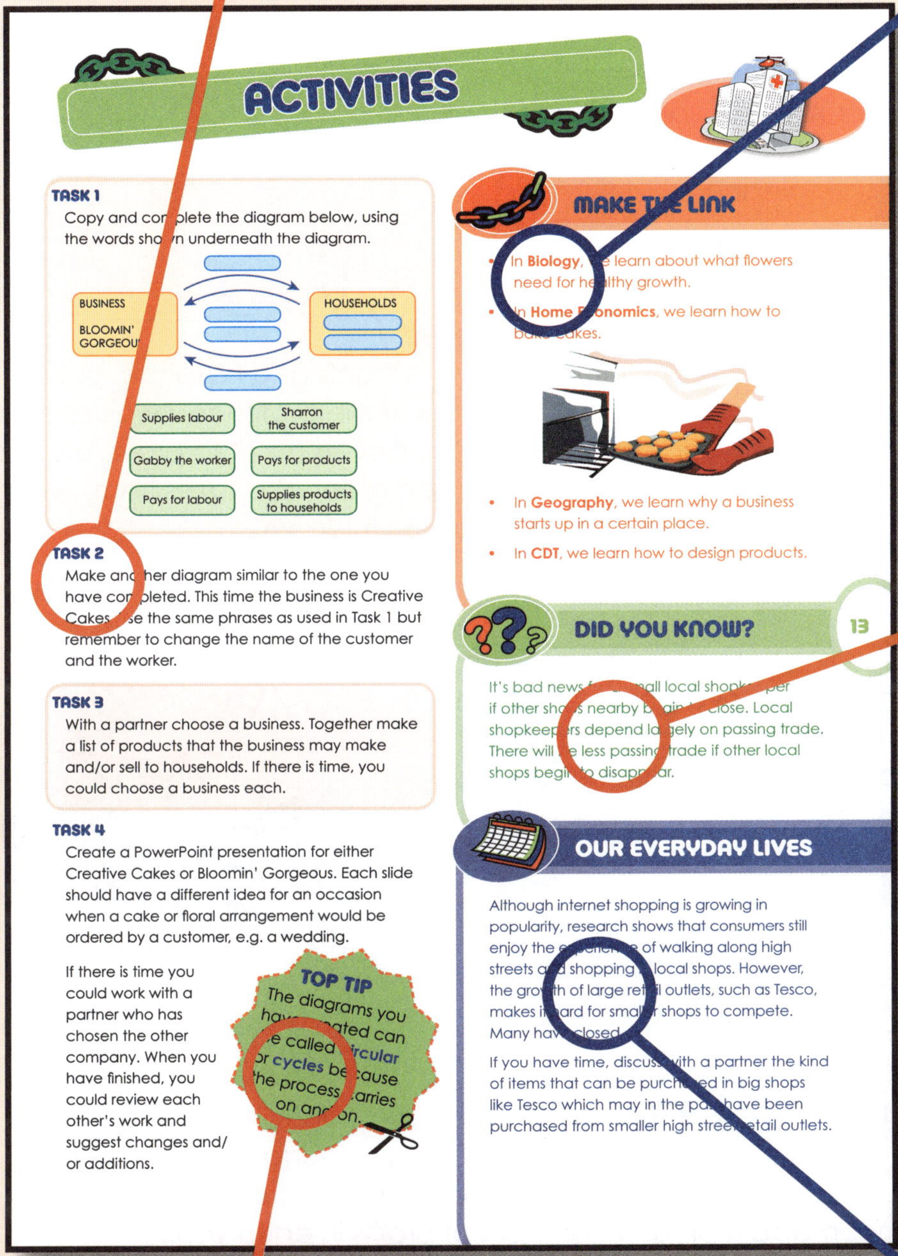
ACTIVITIES

TASK 1
Copy and con plete the diagram below, using the words sho n underneath the diagram.

TASK 2
Make and her diagram similar to the one you have con pleted. This time the business is Creative Cakes se the same phrases as used in Task 1 but remember to change the name of the customer and the worker.

TASK 3
With a partner choose a business. Together make a list of products that the business may make and/or sell to households. If there is time, you could choose a business each.

TASK 4
Create a PowerPoint presentation for either Creative Cakes or Bloomin' Gorgeous. Each slide should have a different idea for an occasion when a cake or floral arrangement would be ordered by a customer, e.g. a wedding.

If there is time you could work with a partner who has chosen the other company. When you have finished, you could review each other's work and suggest changes and/or additions.

TOP TIP
The diagrams you hav ated can e called rcular or cycles be cause the process arries on an on.

MAKE THE LINK
- In Biology, e learn about what flowers need for he thy growth.
- n Home E onomics, we learn how to b cakes.
- In Geography, we learn why a business starts up in a certain place.
- In CDT, we learn how to design products.

DID YOU KNOW? 13
It's bad news f all local shopk per if other sh s nearby b in close. Local shopkeep rs depend la gely on passing trade. There will e less passin trade if other local shops begi o disapp ar.

OUR EVERYDAY LIVES
Although internet shopping is growing in popularity, research shows that consumers still enjoy the e of walking along high streets a shopping local shops. However, the gro th of large ret l outlets, such as Tesco, makes i ard for smal r shops to compete. Many hav closed.

If you have time, discuss ith a partner the kind of items that can be purch ed in big shops like Tesco which may in the pa have been purchased from smaller high stree etail outlets.

DID YOU KNOW?
boxes provide interesting and engaging facts about each topic to help build knowledge

OUR EVERYDAY LIVES
Illustrates how the knowledge translates into practical examples drawn from real life

TOP TIP
Key facts and concepts are highlighted to aid knowledge retention

OUR ECONOMY

You may have heard people talking about 'the economy'. You may have wondered what this means. Quite simply, our economy is everything available to us, such as natural resources and workers, and what we do with it all. The UK economy is just one example of an economy.

Our economy is made up of different parts:

THE PRIVATE SECTOR

This part of our economy consists of people putting finance into business in the hope of making profits. This can be as large as companies like Marks & Spencer or Microsoft. On the other hand, it can be a local shop or a window cleaner.

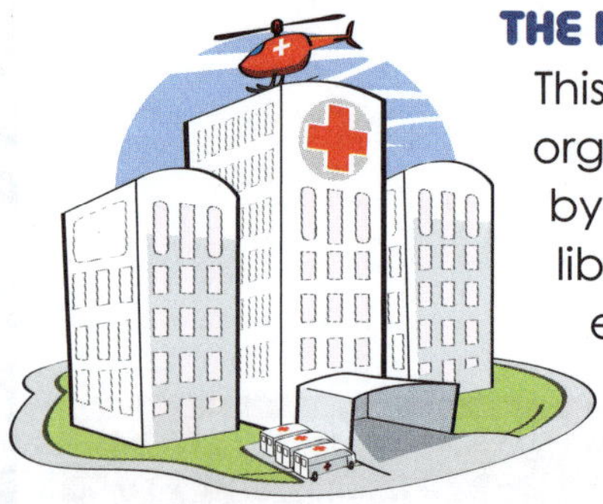

THE PUBLIC SECTOR

This part of our economy consists of organisations that are run and controlled by the government. This includes most schools and hospitals, public libraries and road maintenance. Some of the profits and wages earned in all sectors are taken by the government to provide these services. We call this 'tax'. The government also taxes items we buy and raises finance in that way, for example VAT.

THE VOLUNTARY SECTOR

This part of our economy consists of charities, such as Oxfam, aiming to raise awareness and finance for a good cause. The voluntary sector also includes organisations not existing to make a profit but rather to provide a service for members. A good example is a local tennis club.

EXAMPLE

Kleen & Eezee is a small business owned and run by Caroline Todd and Gina Hislop. Caroline and Gina provide a service for paying customers. They undertake house cleaning and will also do laundry and small amounts of grocery shopping on request. The company has existed since 2006 and has made a pleasing amount of profits in each year.

Caroline and Gina share their profits equally on which they pay tax. They employ David Walker to carry out financial and administration work in the business. David owns no part of the business but is a valued employee who is paid a fair wage.

Caroline donates a certain amount to Barnardo's each month, a charity dear to her heart.

Last year, there was a small fire in the office of the business. The local fire service attended and the fire was extinguished promptly. The owners of the business were able to claim through their insurance company for the damage caused by the fire.

ACTIVITIES

TASK 1

Identify:

1. an organisation in the private sector
2. an organisation in the public sector
3. an organisation in the voluntary sector.

TASK 2

1. Identify two ways in which the government collects tax.
2. Identify whether these tax payments are tax on earnings or tax on spending.

TASK 3

1. Identify the example of a service from the public sector used by Kleen & Eezee.
2. With a partner, make a list of other public services which may be used by a company like Kleen & Eezee.

TASK 4

Caroline donates to Barnardo's, a children's charity. With a partner, carry out research on four other charities. You should choose two charities each. Describe the cause which each charity aims to help. The following headings may help you:

- Charity name
- When it was founded
- Who it aims to help
- Any well-known supporters.

If you have time, you could choose a charity each and turn your research into a PowerPoint presentation to be shown at a later time.

TOP TIP

Public sector workers are paid by the government from tax raised. However, like workers in other sectors, public sector workers also pay tax.

MAKE THE LINK

- In **Modern Studies**, we learn about the government and how it provides services for citizens.
- In **RME**, we learn about charities and their important role in providing for those in need.

DID YOU KNOW?

Although large businesses are usually much more familiar to us, we very much depend on small businesses to make our economy work.

If you have time, you could carry out some research into a popular business near to where you live. For example, you could find out when the business started; if it is the only one in existence or if there are other branches, perhaps in other towns; the names of the owners of the business and if they are local to the area. This information may be available online but you may also consider writing a letter to the business asking if they would mind supplying you with the information.

OUR EVERYDAY LIVES

Successful companies, used to making high levels of profits, have been affected greatly by problems in our economy in recent times – and by other factors. Ryanair, the well-known bargain airline, saw its profits fall considerably in 2010 due to problems caused by the Icelandic volcanic ash cloud.

INTERDISCIPLINARY PROJECT

OUR ECONOMY

No matter which sector an organisation is part of, it will matter to the organisation that it is recognisable to and used by the public.

- In the private sector, more recognisable companies are used more by consumers and make more profits.
- In public sector organisations, such as a public library, it is important to be well known, otherwise the service will not be well used and its funding could be withdrawn.
- In voluntary sector organisations, especially charities, donations are very important for survival. Donations will be higher if the public is aware of the organisation.

Organisations have logos – recognisable symbols – to raise their profile.

EXAMPLE

David Anderson and Cheryl Reilly searched on the internet for different organisations' logos. In the **private sector**, they chose RBS and Boots. In the **public sector**, they chose the Scottish National Blood Transfusion Service and Forestry Commission Scotland. In the **voluntary sector**, they chose two charities, Save the Children and the SSPCA. David and Cheryl divided the work. Together, they agreed on their choice of organisations and, once they had found the logos, they copied and coloured three logos each.

Once completed, David and Cheryl laminated their logos. Their classmates carried out the same task. Their teacher allowed each pair in turn to show their logos to the rest of the class. Classmates were asked to identify, not only the name of the organisation, but also its sector. It was interesting to see how many others in the class recognised the various logos and got the sector right.

Later, some of the logos were displayed on the classroom wall under the headings of the three sectors.

This would be a good task for your class to carry out. Once you have decided on your logos, the drawing and colouring task could be done as a piece of homework. Alternatively, this is a task which could be done in an art lesson. The internet is convenient but don't forget, logos appear in other places, such as newspapers, publicity leaflets and on carrier bags.

MAKE THE LINK

- We learn about the art of letter writing in English.
- We learn about charities and how they depend on donations in RME and other subjects.

ACTIVITIES

TASK 1

Charities form an important part of the voluntary sector. With a partner, choose **two** charities to write to. The charities could be local to your area, national or even international. Together, decide how your letters should be worded. Once this has been agreed, you can each write to one charity.

It would be interesting to find out what the charities set out to achieve but you might have other ideas about what you would like to ask. Remember also that a polite and well-written letter is much more likely to get a response. The examples below may help you to start your letter.
Paragraph 1 might start with: *We are students at ________ High School and are writing to ask you…*
Paragraph 2 might start with: *In particular, we would like to know…*

TASK 2

Answer the following questions:

1. Cheryl and David chose the Scottish National Blood Transfusion Service as one of their organisations from the public sector.
   a. Funding (money) is required to run this service. Suggest where this funding comes from.
   b. Suggest who decides on the amount of funding this organisation will get.
2. Cheryl and David chose Boots as one of their organisations from the private sector.
   a. Who is entitled to a share of the profits made by organisations in the private sector?
   b. Suggest another large retail organisation in the private sector in competition with Boots.
3. Cheryl and David chose Save the Children as an organisation from the voluntary sector.
   a. Suggest different ways in which Save the Children raises funds.
   b. Suggest an example of an organisation in the voluntary sector which is **not** a charity.

MY LEARNING CHECKLIST

Put a tick in the column to show how you think you got on with each statement.
Green means you got on really well with your learning in this area.
Amber means you did well with your learning.
Red means you need to do a bit of work on your learning.

	Statement	Good to go!	Getting there	Help needed
1.	*I understand that our economy is divided into three areas (or sectors). I know the names of each sector.*	○	○	○
2.	*I understand the types of organisations in each sector and how they are funded.*	○	○	○
3.	*I understand what organisations in each sector set out to achieve (aims).*	○	○	○
4.	*I understand that organisations vary in size from the smallest corner shop to large organisations like Microsoft.*	○	○	○
5.	*I understand the importance to an organisation of having a recognisable logo.*	○	○	○

BUSINESSES TO HOUSEHOLDS AND HOUSEHOLDS TO BUSINESSES

Almost every business we can think of **depends on people who work** in that business. Without them, the business would not be able to continue. Businesses also **depend on people who buy their products**.

However, at the same time, **people depend on businesses**. They depend on businesses to **make and sell all the products they want to buy**. Equally, they depend on **businesses to give them jobs** so that they can earn money to buy products.

Therefore, we can see that businesses and people (households) depend on each other for a busy and successful economy.

EXAMPLE

Bloomin' Gorgeous is a successful florist shop in the Scottish Borders. It specialises in wedding bouquets. Gabby Barnes has worked in the shop as a trainee florist for twelve months. Gabby is getting married in the near future.

Sharron Begg works as a baker in the shop next door to Bloomin' Gorgeous, Creative Cakes. Sharron is also getting married very soon.

You won't be surprised to learn that Gabby has ordered her wedding cake from Creative Cakes and Sharron has ordered her bouquets from Bloomin' Gorgeous.

ACTIVITIES

TASK 1

Copy and complete the diagram below, using the words shown underneath the diagram.

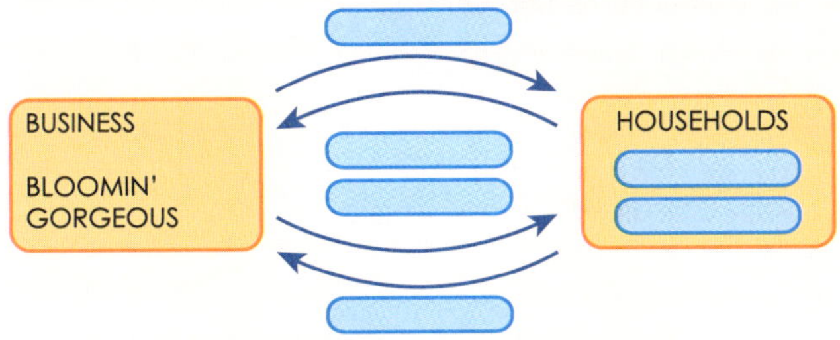

- Supplies labour
- Sharron the customer
- Gabby the worker
- Pays for products
- Pays for labour
- Supplies products to households

TASK 2

Make another diagram similar to the one you have completed. This time the business is Creative Cakes. Use the same phrases as used in Task 1 but remember to change the name of the customer and the worker.

TASK 3

With a partner choose a business. Together make a list of products that the business may make and/or sell to households. If there is time, you could choose a business each.

TASK 4

Create a PowerPoint presentation for either Creative Cakes or Bloomin' Gorgeous. Each slide should have a different idea for an occasion when a cake or floral arrangement would be ordered by a customer, e.g. a wedding.

If there is time you could work with a partner who has chosen the other company. When you have finished, you could review each other's work and suggest changes and/or additions.

TOP TIP

The diagrams you have created can be called **circular** or **cycles** because the process carries on and on.

MAKE THE LINK

- In **Biology**, we learn about what flowers need for healthy growth.
- In **Home Economics**, we learn how to bake cakes.

- In **Geography**, we learn why a business starts up in a certain place.
- In **CDT**, we learn how to design products.

DID YOU KNOW?

It's bad news for a small local shopkeeper if other shops nearby begin to close. Local shopkeepers depend largely on passing trade. There will be less passing trade if other local shops begin to disappear.

OUR EVERYDAY LIVES

Although internet shopping is growing in popularity, research shows that consumers still enjoy the experience of walking along high streets and shopping in local shops. However, the growth of large retail outlets, such as Tesco, makes it hard for smaller shops to compete. Many have closed.

If you have time, discuss with a partner the kind of items that can be purchased in big shops like Tesco which may in the past have been purchased from smaller high street retail outlets.

INTERDISCIPLINARY PROJECT

BUSINESSES TO HOUSEHOLDS AND HOUSEHOLDS TO BUSINESSES

We know that businesses need households and households need businesses – but there is more to it than simply supplying each other with what is needed. Consider this example.

EXAMPLE

John Wyse lives in a small village. He doesn't venture far from home because he works as a blacksmith's assistant in the village and the local shop supplies most of his needs. The blacksmith pays John enough to cover his living costs – and a bit more besides.

Like many other people, John has to pay tax on his earnings. This means that not all of his pay can be spent at the local shop because the government takes some of it away from him. Also, John saves some of his earnings, so again the local shop doesn't get that part of his earnings. Furthermore, John likes going online and buying items from other countries. That means even more of his earnings do not go to the local shop.

However, it's not all bad news. Money also flows back into the circular flow:

- At least some of the tax John pays finds its way back into our economy because the government uses John's taxes, for example on road-building.
- Businesses spend too: for example, when the blacksmith buys a new anvil or other piece of equipment.
- Businesses in this country don't just sell to us, they also sell to people abroad.

This task involves making a feature for your classroom wall. If you are artistic, you could draw or point John. Show images representing John's spending and show an arrow from John to each image. If you have time you could make another feature showing John's tax and outward arrows showing what his tax is spent on. Instead of drawing John and the images, you could cut out images from magazines and paste them on.

MAKE THE LINK

- We learn about the work of government in **Modern Studies**.
- We learn about the benefits of saving in **Social Education**.

ACTIVITIES

TASK 1

The following six reasons explain why money either enters or leaves the circular flow:

- imports
- government spending
- exports
- savings
- tax
- investment by industry.

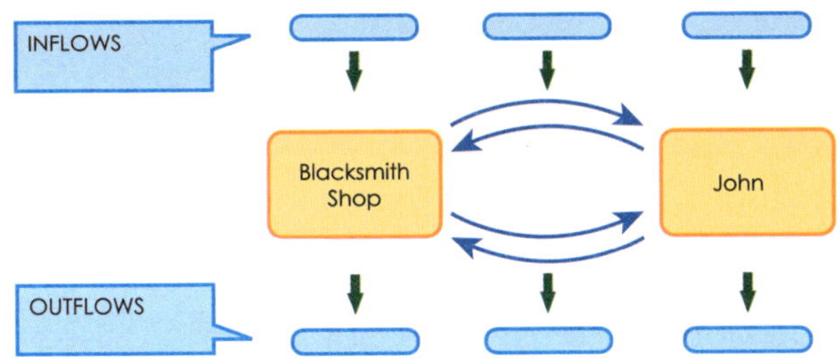

Draw the diagram and add these reasons as either **inflows** or **outflows**.

TASK 2

Carry out the following tasks:

1. John pays income tax. Make a list of all the services you can think of which are made possible by people like John paying income tax.
2. Income tax is just one example of a tax. Visit three or four teachers (or perhaps you can ask people at home instead) and ask about other kinds of taxes that are paid. You could compete with your classmates to see who can get the highest number of taxes.
3. Many people save some of their pay.
   a. Suggest reasons why people save.
   b. Suggest why a low interest rate at the bank may discourage saving.

MY LEARNING CHECKLIST

Put a tick in the column to show how you think you got on with each statement.
Green means you got on really well with your learning in this area.
Amber means you did well with your learning.
Red means you need to do a bit of work on your learning.

	Statement	Good to go!	Getting there	Help needed
1.	*I understand that money flows from households to businesses and businesses to households.*	◯	◯	◯
2.	*I understand that some money flows out of the circular flow and I can give examples of those money flows.*	◯	◯	◯
3.	*I understand that some money flows into the circular flow and I can give examples of those money flows.*	◯	◯	◯
4.	*I understand that there are different taxes and how the government spends the tax.*	◯	◯	◯
5.	*I understand why businesses need to spend and I can give examples of what a business might buy.*	◯	◯	◯

TYPES OF BUSINESSES – THE SOLE TRADER

Businesses range in sizes, from very small to very large. A business can be owned by a large number of people but in some cases there may be only one owner.

A business with only one owner is called a **sole trader**.

The sole trader may work alongside others in the business but they will be the only person who owns it. Therefore, only that person will be entitled to the profits made by the business. At the same time, however, if the business loses money, the sole trader will be responsible for the loss. In fact, a sole trader going out of business leaving debts could be sued for their personal possessions, such as their house. This is because they do not have **limited liability**.

While he or she is free to take advice from others, only the sole trader will make final decisions on matters affecting the business.

EXAMPLE

Gareth Thornton trained as a barber ten years ago. Since then, Gareth has operated as a sole trader in his small shop on the outskirts of Glasgow.

Although Gareth has been happy in his shop, he is considering joining forces with his sister-in-law, Fiona Thornton, who is an experienced ladies' hair stylist. He believes that the business will be more successful if both male and female hair styling is offered. Also, Fiona is offering to invest £15 000 in the business, which would mean they would be able to move to larger premises and buy more up-to-date equipment to add to the appeal of the business.

TOP TIP
Although there is very little paperwork involved in setting up as a sole trader, the new businessperson must let the tax authorities know about their intention to start in business.

Gareth's wife, Elaine, does not think Gareth should go into business with Fiona. She says she doesn't think the business will make enough profit to share between two people. She also worries about disagreements arising between Gareth and Fiona on business decisions.

ACTIVITIES

TASK 1

With a partner, make a list of the points of view (for and against) of both Gareth and Elaine. Take into consideration all the points made in the passage and any other points you may consider to be important. Based on your discussion, decide whether or not Gareth and Fiona should go into business together. Be ready to tell your class what you think they should do – and why you believe this.

TASK 2

Gareth could offer to take Fiona on as an employee in the business, in which case she would be paid a wage but would not own any part of the business.

1. With your partner, write down an advantage and a disadvantage of this **for Fiona**.
2. With your partner, write down an advantage and a disadvantage of this **for Gareth**.

TASK 3

Make a list of businesses that you believe would operate well as sole traders. Compare your list with your partner's. How many ideas appear in both lists? Discuss between you why you think the businesses you have both picked would work well as sole traders.

TASK 4

If Gareth and Fiona work together, there will be more variety in what they offer customers. We call this 'diversification'. Make a PowerPoint presentation containing other services that could be offered by this business.

1. Include a slide on why it might be a good idea to offer a range of services.
2. Include a slide on any drawbacks of offering a range of services rather than just concentrating on one or two services.

   Be ready to speak about this in a class discussion.

MAKE THE LINK

- In **CDT** – we learn about newly developed products and the benefits of well-designed products.
- In **Maths** – we learn how to calculate the percentage of profit made on an investment.

DID YOU KNOW?

Although it would not be impossible for a large company to be a sole trader, it would be unusual. In most cases, the amount invested in a company is much less if only one owner is investing. Usually, when a second or third owner joins a business, it can grow in size as there is more money to invest.

OUR EVERYDAY LIVES

In recent times, we have seen many people lose their jobs due to difficult economic circumstances. Often people losing their jobs will receive a sum of money to compensate for their loss of job. This is called 'redundancy pay'. Sometimes a person losing their job will use this money to start in business. In many cases, it has only been the fear of giving up a job – and perhaps a lack of finance – which has stopped them from becoming their own boss. It can be their new unemployed status that gives them the push towards self-employment.

Perhaps you could ask someone at home – or maybe some of your other teachers – if anyone has any knowledge of businesses which have started due to the owner or owners being made redundant.

INTERDISCIPLINARY PROJECT

TYPES OF BUSINESSES – THE SOLE TRADER

Sole trading organisations tend to be small businesses. Although there is definitely a place for small businesses in our economy, the risk of failing is higher for a small business because:

- The small business carries a **bigger risk** so will find it difficult to get banks to lend money. This can be the difference between surviving and failing.
- The **costs** of operating as a small business are higher. For example, buying in smaller quantities of stock will mean a higher price for that stock.
- It can be hard to stay in business if a larger, better-known business is in **competition**.

Many people nowadays are very health-conscious and want to eat healthy food. The government carries out campaigns to encourage everyone to think about what they eat. With this in mind, you and your partner have been asked to come up with a range of takeaway food for a new business, Healthy Heaven. The food can be hot or cold or a mixture. About ten to twelve items for the menu are required. Be careful that the food on your takeaway menu is reasonably low in calories, sugar and fat. However, this is a business hoping to attract customers so the food must have lunchtime appeal.

You will have to find out:

- the calorie and fat content of food you would like to include on your menu
- the recommended daily intake of calories and fat for men and women.

Don't forget, however, that this is a business and being healthy cannot be at the expense of making a profit. Therefore you will have to find out:

- the kind of food people want to eat at lunchtime
- how much it will cost to make a lunchtime dish and how much it will sell for.

All of the above will require you to carry out research. This can be online research but you may consider preparing questionnaires to ask people their opinions. Don't forget that you have an excellent source of information in the school – the Home Economics department.

MAKE THE LINK

- We learn about the benefits of living a healthy lifestyle in **Home Economics** and **PE**.

ACTIVITIES

TASK 1

Getting the name of a business right is very important. You may not think Healthy Heaven is a good name for the business. Can you and your partner come up with a better name?

It will have to be **a name which is individual enough to stand out** on a high street but at the same time it will have to **relate to the products being sold**. If you come up with a few possibilities, you could carry out research to find out which name is the most popular.

You could also make a logo for the business using your chosen name.

TASK 2

Answer the following questions:

1. Large and small businesses know that they are likely to have competition. In the case of Healthy Heaven:
   a. Suggest a well-known business which may be Healthy Heaven's competition.
   b. Suggest what Healthy Heaven could do to win customers away from the competitor.
2. The owner of Healthy Heaven may need to borrow funds.
   a. Make a list of well-known banks the owner of Healthy Heaven could apply to for a loan.
   b. Suggest other options for raising funds for a business like Healthy Heaven.
3. Healthy Heaven will open as a retail outlet on a busy high street.
   a. Suggest any disadvantages of setting up in this location.
   b. Suggest other ways the business could sell products.

MY LEARNING CHECKLIST

Put a tick in the column to show how you think you got on with each statement.
Green means you got on really well with your learning in this area.
Amber means you did well with your learning.
Red means you need to do a bit of work on your learning.

	Statement	Good to go!	Getting there	Help needed
1.	*I know the number of owners in a sole trading business.*			
2.	*I understand the problems that could arise from being a sole trader.*			
3.	*I understand that a sole trading business is likely to be a small business.*			
4.	*I understand that small businesses face problems which larger businesses experience less.*			
5.	*I understand the importance of getting the name of a company right.*			
6.	*I understand why healthy eating is encouraged by the government.*			

TYPES OF BUSINESSES – PARTNERSHIPS

We have learned about single business owners, known as sole traders. A sole trader may, however, decide to go into business with another (or others) and become a **partnership**.

The partners in a partnership will all invest money (also known as **capital**) in the business but not necessarily in equal amounts. Profits (or loss) made by the partners will be shared but again this does not have to be in equal parts. Sometimes the share of the profit each partner receives is based on how much capital that partner invested in the business, but this is not always the case. For example, one partner might not have invested a great deal of capital, but may invest the highest number of hours working in the business.

TOP TIP

It may seem like a good idea to go into partnership – but it is important to think first. Many partnerships fail because of personality clashes. You don't have to be best friends but you do need a good working relationship and respect for each other's opinions. Think about what partners might fall out about.

Often, partners in a business will draw up a **deed of partnership** which sets out everything that has been agreed between the partners. Matters such as how profits are shared and other important points, like holiday entitlement, are included in this document. Like sole traders, a partnership does not have the benefit of **limited liability**.

EXAMPLE

The barber, Gareth Thornton, spoke to his neighbour, Ray Kennedy, about going into partnership. Ray has experience of this because he used to be a sole trader, working as a painter and decorator, but two years ago he went into partnership with a carpenter and an electrician with the idea of offering a range of services to customers.

ACTIVITIES

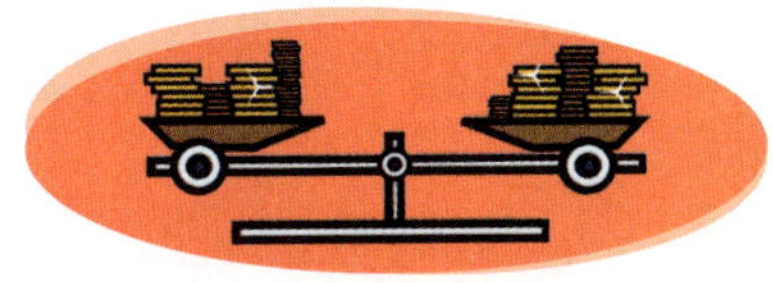

TASK 1

Discuss with a partner the benefits to Ray and his two partners of being in partnership. One of you should make a note of everything you have discussed. You should also discuss any drawbacks for Ray and his partners. This could be turned into a presentation later.

TASK 2

Imagine you are buying a house which is in a very poor state of repair and needs everything done. You could hire the services of Ray and his partners – but perhaps there are other services which would be necessary to refurbish the house. Discuss with your partner other services which would ideally be offered by Ray's company. Don't just think about the outside of the building – think about the inside too. Once you have decided on what would be done, turn your decisions into a PowerPoint presentation. It would be a good idea to divide the work to be done into two parts, e.g. inside the house and outside the house, so that you can each create a PowerPoint presentation.

TASK 3

Make a list of important points that you think should be included in a deed of partnership. This may be used in class discussion later.

TASK 4

Ray and his partners have put the same amount of capital into the business and work a similar number of hours. Therefore, they decided to share the profits equally.

1. Last year they made a profit of £74 862. How much did each partner receive?
2. If it had been decided that Ray should get half of the profits and the others should share the remainder between them, how much would Ray get and how much would the others get?

MAKE THE LINK

- In **CDT**, we learn about how tasks are planned and completed.
- In **Maths**, we learn how to calculate the amount each partner will receive.

DID YOU KNOW?

According to http://www.businesslink.gov.uk, in a partnership each partner is responsible for the debts of the partnership as a whole. This means that each partner's personal assets may be at risk if the business fails.

OUR EVERYDAY LIVES

Most of us are familiar with a business called the John Lewis Partnership which has stores throughout the UK. Although described as a partnership, it is actually owned by a trust who act on behalf of the employees (known as partners). The partners do get a share of the profits, on top of their yearly salary, but they are not involved in the day-to-day decision-making of the famous store.

INTERDISCIPLINARY PROJECT

TYPES OF BUSINESSES – PARTNERSHIPS

When thinking about expansion, a sole trader may well consider going into partnership. Apart from the obvious benefit of increasing the capital so the business can grow, the possibility of offering consumers a more diverse range of products may seem like a good idea for the following reasons:

- Offering a diverse product range can give the consumer a 'one stop shop' for all their needs.
- A range of products will reduce the risk in case one of the products loses popularity.
- The goodwill built up around one product may well transfer to other products being offered.

Healthy Heaven has been in business for some time and is doing well. The business is at present owned by one person, Ruth Reilly. However, Ruth's employee, Bridget Stevens, is a qualified Pilates instructor and it has been decided that they will form a partnership, with Bridget teaching Pilates classes. In order to do this, they have rented premises nearby with more floor space. The floor space will be used as a sit-in health café but is flexible so the tables and chairs can be easily collapsed and the space can be made suitable for Pilates.

You and your partner have been asked to give Ruth and Bridget advice to help them get started in their new improved business.

Your advice for Ruth and Bridget could be in a PowerPoint presentation. For at least some of the advice, you will be required to carry out research.

- **Slide 1** should be an introduction slide including your names.

Although Ruth and Bridget have a good working relationship, they are concerned that business partners often have disagreements.

- In **slide 2** give advice on likely reasons for disagreement.

Ruth and Bridget realise they should have a **deed of partnership** (**partnership agreement**).

- In **slide 3** give Ruth and Bridget advice on what should be included in the deed.

The two women are unsure about whether to keep or change the business name. They believe there are reasons to keep the original name; on the other hand, there might be advantages in choosing something else.

- In **slide 4** state why the original name should be changed or kept.
- In **slide 5** give Ruth and Bridget advice on café opening times and Pilates class times.

You have also decided to offer Ruth and Bridget advice on further diversification for the business in the future. Think about other business possibilities which would work well with the healthy food and Pilates classes.

ACTIVITIES

TASK 1

Ruth and Bridget would be wise to prepare a schedule stating when the business will be open for takeaway, sit-in food and Pilates. This could be designed in the form of a four-page leaflet, two pages on one side of a sheet of A4 paper and the other two pages on the other side. Having decided on when in the week the business will be open for each of the services, prepare a four-page leaflet for customers to keep.

TASK 2

Answer the following questions:

1. Businesses nowadays commonly have a website.
   a. Suggest reasons why they might benefit from having a website.
   b. Suggest what the business might include in their website.
2. The partners may or may not split their profits equally.
   a. Suggest reasons why they may **not** split the profits 50 : 50.
   b. Suggest reasons why their profit split may change in the future.
3. If Ruth and Bridget make a clear profit of £48 942 in their first year:
   a. state how much they would each get if the split was 50 : 50
   b. state how much they would get if the split was 60 : 40 (Ruth 60 and Bridget 40).

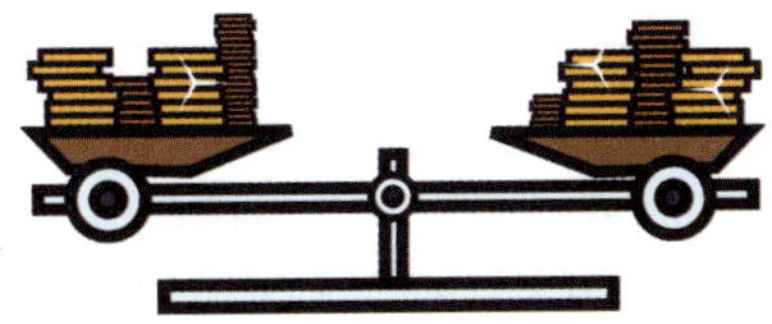

MY LEARNING CHECKLIST

Put a tick in the column to show how you think you got on with each statement.
Green means you got on really well with your learning in this area.
Amber means you did well with your learning.
Red means you need to do a bit of work on your learning.

	Good to go!	Getting there	Help needed
1. I know that partners do not always share the profits equally.			
2. I understand why partnerships may not always work out well.			
3. I understand why a sole trading business may see becoming a partnership as an attractive prospect.			
4. I understand why it is wise to have a deed of partnership.			
5. I understand how to calculate the division of profits based on an agreed split, such as 50 : 50 or 60 : 40.			

TYPES OF BUSINESSES – PRIVATE LIMITED COMPANIES

A private limited company is an organisation with its finance (capital) supplied by its owners. These owners are called **shareholders** because they all own a share of the business. It will be decided who the shareholders will be and only these people will be entitled to own shares in the business.

Often a business which was previously a partnership will decide to become a private limited company. They may decide on this type of business because they are keen for only their existing owners to be shareholders. They may also wish to move away from being a partnership because they want the benefit of **limited liability**, meaning that all they can lose if the business fails is their investment in the business.

TOP TIP

In Wales, a different word can be used instead of 'Limited' or 'Ltd' after the business name. You could try to find out what the word is, although you probably won't be able to pronounce it!

EXAMPLE

For a few years, Sarah Blackmore was a partner in a dog-grooming parlour. For various reasons, the business began to fail and, when it eventually closed, it left a great deal of debt, including to several suppliers. Sarah, as a partner, was liable for part of the debt left by the failed business. Understandably, Sarah vowed never to go into business again.

Had the dog-grooming parlour been a private limited company, all Sarah would have lost was the amount of capital she invested in the company. Of course, she would have lost the money she invested, but at least she wouldn't have been liable for anything else.

ACTIVITIES

TASK 1

Carry out some research to find private limited companies. You may choose to do this with a partner. It would be good to find companies you recognise but if you find some which are less familiar to you, that will be interesting too.
Find out what the business supplies, how long it has been around and anything else you consider to be interesting. You may find out that the business used to be a partnership or a sole trader. You could present your findings in a table.

TASK 2

A private limited company must by law include the word **Limited** (or alternatively **Ltd**) after its name and its registered office must appear on its business letterhead. Choose a business name (real or imagined) for a private limited company. Design a letterhead for the company, including a company logo, to be used on all the company's correspondence.

TASK 3

Most businesses depend on suppliers allowing them to pay on credit, meaning that they pay some time after receiving the supplies.

1. Write a paragraph explaining the benefits to a company of buying on credit.
2. Write another paragraph explaining the danger to the suppliers of allowing credit sales.

TASK 4

Four people decide to go into business together as a private limited company. They have decided they need capital of £180 000. Andrew and Brian will each hold 30% of the shares. Charlotte will hold 25% of the shares.

1. David is the fourth shareholder. What would his percentage shareholding be?
2. What is the value of the shares held by each shareholder?

MAKE THE LINK

- In **Social Education**, we learn about buying on credit and the danger of building up too much debt.
- In **Maths**, we learn about percentages and how percentages relate to values.

DID YOU KNOW?

It's not uncommon for an employee to become a shareholder in a company. An employee may be offered the chance to buy shares in the company or even be given free shares.

Reasons for an employer offering employees the chance to become shareholders would be an interesting topic for class discussion.

OUR EVERYDAY LIVES

Often consumers buy on credit. Retailers see offering credit as an incentive to consumers who might otherwise not be able (or willing) to buy products. Low – or even zero – interest will make the offer even more attractive. Some retailers even offer deals like 'pay nothing for six months' to attract customers. This can cause problems for retailers in the long run if their customers have trouble paying on the due date.

INTERDISCIPLINARY PROJECT

TYPES OF BUSINESSES – PRIVATE LIMITED COMPANIES

Perhaps in the future Ruth and Bridget may consider becoming a private limited company:

- They may be more prepared to invest in their business if they are protected by limited liability.
- They may be keen to bring in more investors who would be attracted to a limited company.
- Ruth and Bridget may wish to keep control of their company.

You and your partner want to convince Ruth and Bridget that becoming a private limited company may be a good option for the future. Look at the list of companies below. All the companies on the list are private limited companies. Choose a company and prepare a presentation based on your choice of company. Your aim is to show Ruth and Bridget how a private limited company can be successful. Choose from the list of private limited companies, or perhaps you have another option of your own.

1. Cameron Mackintosh Limited
2. Warburtons Limited
3. Russell Hobbs Limited
4. Spar (UK) Limited
5. Jewson Limited
6. BAA Airports Limited
7. Northern Bank Limited
8. Timpson Limited
9. DC Thomson & Co. Limited

Having researched your choice, include in your presentation: the name of the company, its registered number, where it is registered, its products, information about its background/history and any other interesting information you can find about the company. You could present your work to the rest of your class, so it would be a good idea to choose different companies.

MAKE THE LINK

- We learn about laws and how they exist to protect us in **Modern Studies**.

ACTIVITIES

TASK 1

If Ruth and Bridget decide that becoming a private limited company is a good idea, they will have to register their proposed company name. Once you have what you consider a good name for the company, check if the name is available. If another company has the name, you will have to think of an alternative. The website to use is: http://www.duport.co.uk/company-formation.

TASK 2

Answer the following questions:

1. Business investors see limited liability as an advantage.
   a. Explain the attraction of limited liability to an investor.
   b. Suggest types of business organisations which **do not** have limited liability.
2. Shareholders in a private limited company can only sell their shares to an authorised shareholder in the company and with the directors' permission.
   a. Suggest why this may stop an investor from investing in a private limited company.
   b. Suggest why shareholders might not want an outside investor to be able to buy shares in the company.
3. If the shares in the company are presently valued at £6·40 and next year they are worth £9·60:
   a. calculate the percentage rise in the share price over the year
   b. suggest what might have caused the share price to rise and what might cause the share price to fall.

HELPFUL HINT

The following formula calculates a percentage change:

$$\frac{\text{Difference between original number and number after change}}{\text{Original number}} \times 100$$

MY LEARNING CHECKLIST

Put a tick in the column to show how you think you got on with each statement.
Green means you got on really well with your learning in this area.
Amber means you did well with your learning.
Red means you need to do a bit of work on your learning.

	Good to go!	Getting there	Help needed
1. *I understand the concept of limited liability.*	○	○	○
2. *I understand that private limited companies must be registered and cannot register under the same name as another registered company.*	○	○	○
3. *I understand that the value of shares can rise and fall.*	○	○	○
4. *I can express a rise or fall in the price of shares as a percentage.*	○	○	○
5. *I understand that shares in a private limited company cannot be sold to investors outside the company without the consent of the directors.*	○	○	○

TYPES OF BUSINESSES – PUBLIC LIMITED COMPANIES

A public limited company (plc) is also an organisation with its capital supplied by its owners (shareholders). However, in the case of a public limited company, it is possible to have many more shareholders than in a private limited company. This is because a public limited company's shares are available to buy and sell on the Stock Market.

Almost anyone can own shares in a public limited company. This means that the company can raise a lot more capital, so can grow in size more easily. This is considered to be a big advantage of becoming a public limited company.

TOP TIP

If you own shares in a limited company and the company makes profits, you will receive a share of the profits. We call this a **share dividend**.

Just like a private limited company, shareholders in a public limited company benefit from **limited liability**.

EXAMPLE

Scottish-based company Farmfoods Limited started trading in 1954. It has its headquarters in Lanarkshire. The company began as a meat manufacturer but, over time, it expanded into retail and now can be seen in many locations across the UK as a retailer of frozen foods and other grocery items.

The company is still a private limited company. This means it can restrict its share ownership and avoid being taken over by another larger company. The benefit of more capital investment does not seem to have tempted Farmfoods to become a public limited company. If the company did become a plc, its shares would be offered for sale on the stock market.

ACTIVITIES

TASK 1

A well-known competitor of Farmfoods is Iceland. Carry out some research to find out:

- the location of the headquarters of Iceland
- if it is a private limited company or a public limited company
- when the company was founded.

TASK 2

Share Certificate

LANCHESTER HOLDINGS PLC

LANCHESTER ROVERS FC

Certificate Number 04210

Date 1 October 2010

This is to certify that the undermentioned is/are the registered Holder(s) of fully paid shares in Lanchester Holdings plc.

Name(s) of Holders	Number of Shares
Gordon Craig	100 Ordinary £1 Shares

Note: This document is valuable. Keep this document in a safe place.

Lanchester Rovers FC was recently **floated**, meaning the club is now a public limited company. Gordon Craig bought 100 shares in the football club. He is a lifelong supporter of the club.

Make a share certificate for a company, either real or invented by you. You could choose a football club but there are many other types of companies you could choose. You could work with a partner on this task. For example, one of you could be working on the logo while the other works on the layout of the certificate.

TASK 3

The shares in Lanchester Holdings were worth £1 each when they were floated. However, some bad publicity in the press about the club and a run of disappointing results have caused the share price to fall to 80 pence.

1. Calculate how much Gordon would receive if he sold his shares for 80 pence each.
2. Calculate the percentage fall in the share price.
3. Calculate the percentage rise in the share price if it had risen from £1 to £1·28.

MAKE THE LINK

- In **Maths**, we learn about percentages and other calculations.
- In **English**, we learn about language and how to write in different styles.

DID YOU KNOW?

A person with a lot of debt they cannot pay may be declared **bankrupt**. If so, that person will not be allowed to buy shares in a public limited company.

OUR EVERYDAY LIVES

You may have seen the letters **plc** after a company name. This tells us that the company is a public limited company and that shares can be bought and sold on the Stock Market.

Can you remember what comes after the name of a private limited company?

TASK 4

Write a short article for a newspaper that would make your company's share price rise. Write in an interesting way that would encourage readers to keep reading. Write a second article, this time about something which would cause the share price to fall. Work with a partner. One partner could work on one news story and the other on the second news story. Review your partner's work. Is there anything you would suggest changing?

INTERDISCIPLINARY PROJECT

TYPES OF BUSINESSES – PUBLIC LIMITED COMPANIES

Many organisations that have started small, perhaps even as sole traders, become public limited companies by floating on the stock market:

- They may see increasing capital by selling shares to more investors as necessary for expansion.
- They may see expansion as a way of moving into other parts of the UK or even overseas.

The **FTSE 100 Share Index** is a list of the most popular companies in the UK in terms of share trading. This changes from time to time as companies gain or lose popularity. For example, a government campaign on the dangers of smoking could cause the shares in a tabacco company to fall. Either alone or with a partner, choose a company from the FTSE 100 Share Index. You may want to do some research on the company before making your choice to see how well the company has been doing lately. Something might make you believe the company is going to grow in popularity. For example, in April 2010 many holidaymakers were dismayed by the disruption to air travel due to the ash cloud. Could such an event cause the share price of a British holiday company, like Butlin's, to rise?

- You have £500 to invest.
- Having chosen your company, take a note of the share price. You will probably find that this is expressed in pence, e.g. 128 pence. You will have to calculate how many shares you can buy with your investment.
- On a regular basis, perhaps once a week, check the share price. Take a note of the share price. Don't be disappointed if it has fallen as you may well find it has risen again the next time you check.
- After two or three months, calculate the value of your shareholding. Do you have more or less than your original £500?

Don't forget, there is always a risk attached to trading in shares.

MAKE THE LINK

- We learn about the dangers of smoking in **Social Education** and in **Science**.
- We use graphs and charts in many subjects, including **Maths**.

ACTIVITIES

TASK 1

Create a line, bar or column chart to show the performance of your shares over the time period. You could add comments below your chart about possible reasons for a rise or fall in the share price at certain times.

TASK 2

Shares on the stock market rise and fall as the result of something a company does or does not do. The rise or fall could also be due to an outside influence. Look at the possible reasons for a change in a share price listed in the table. State whether you think the occurrence would cause a rise or fall in the share price.

Occurrence causing share price change	Share price: up or down
New product found to be of poor quality.	
Competing firm creates a new, popular product.	
Large retailer decides to start stocking the product.	
It is discovered that the company uses child labour in an Asian country.	

TASK 3

Sometimes potential investors are discouraged from investing because of the product a company makes and/or sells or perhaps techniques used to make the product. With a partner, discuss issues which would stop you from buying shares in a company.

Write down why you feel this way. This can be made into a presentation to show to your class. To help you, examples are shown below:

- I would not invest in a company involved in cigarette production because evidence shows that cigarettes are addictive and can cause early death.
- I would not invest in a company involved in testing products on animals as I believe it is cruel.

MY LEARNING CHECKLIST

Put a tick in the column to show how you think you got on with each statement.

Green means you got on really well with your learning in this area.

Amber means you did well with your learning.

Red means you need to do a bit of work on your learning.

	Good to go!	Getting there	Help needed
1. I understand the attraction of floating a company on the stock market.	○	○	○
2. I understand that shares can rise and fall in price for various internal and external reasons.	○	○	○
3. I understand why some people may not want to invest in certain companies, even profitable ones.	○	○	○
4. I understand that companies listed in the FTSE 100 Share Index can change over time.	○	○	○
5. I understand that shares in a public limited company can be sold to any investor who wishes to buy shares in the company.	○	○	○

WHOSE FIRM IS IT ANYWAY?

We have learned about different types and sizes of organisations – but do we know:

- Who owns them?
- Who runs them?
- Who funds them?

EXAMPLE

My name is Louisa Drake. I am a sole trader. I make pottery plates and other items. I feel being a sole trader is right for me. I like being the only person controlling my business, although I do consider the opinions of my only employee, George. As the only person putting money into the business, I feel it is only fair that I am entitled to that privilege.

My name is George Lee. I work for Louisa Drake making pottery items. I would like to be Louisa's business partner and so own part of the business. I could invest my savings in the business. It would be great to be part of the decision-making process.

CHOMP-IT

EXAMPLE

My name is Laura Adams. Along with twenty-five other investors, I am a shareholder in Chomp It Limited, a catering company. I am also one of the directors on the board of the company. The directors make the decisions on behalf of all of the shareholders as it would be too complicated if all shareholders had a say. However, if they don't like what the board does, the shareholders can vote to have us replaced.

One of my fellow directors is keen to float Chomp It Limited on the stock market, but I am not keen. We could end up being taken over by another company.

My name is Lesley Thomson. I too own shares in Chomp It Limited and am on the board of directors. In order to expand the company, I would like it to float on the stock market. That way, we would have many more investors.

TOP TIP

Sell a pottery dish to a customer and you are selling a good. Teach them how to make it and you are selling a service.

ACTIVITIES

TASK 1

Ask your partner the following questions and write down their answers:

1. Who owns the pottery business?
2. Who controls the pottery business?
3. Who funds the pottery business?

Do you agree with your partner's answers? Discuss any differences of opinion you have.

TASK 2

Switch roles. Ask your partner the following questions and write down their answers:

1. Who owns the catering business?
2. Who controls the catering business?
3. Who funds the catering business?

Do you agree with your partner's answers? Discuss any differences of opinion you have.

TASK 3

Switch roles again. Ask your partner the following questions and write down their answers:

1. Who would own the pottery business if George invested?
2. Who would control the pottery business if George invested?
3. Who would fund the pottery business if George invested?

Do you agree with your partner's answers? Discuss any differences of opinion you have.

TASK 4

Switch roles. Ask your partner the following questions and write down their answers:

1. What does Lesley Thomson want for the future of Chomp It Limited?
2. Why is Laura Adams against Lesley's wish?
3. If Lesley gets her way, Chomp It Limited will have a new name. What will this new name be?

Do you agree with your partner's answers? Discuss any differences of opinion you have.

MAKE THE LINK

- We learn about pottery and clay in **Art and Design**.

DID YOU KNOW?

We assume that large companies have been floated on the stock market to help expansion, but even big companies like Virgin remain private limited companies. You could do some research to find out about other companies choosing not to float on the stock market.

OUR EVERYDAY LIVES

Making pots and similar crafts can be considered to be therapeutic. Nowadays, businesses offering to let customers make their own pots, with instruction and supervision, can be found around the country.

INTERDISCIPLINARY PROJECT

WHOSE FIRM IS IT ANYWAY?

We know that not all owners of organisations are necessarily involved in the running of their organisations.

- A sole trader, as the only owner, will be in charge of running the company. Others may assist the sole trader in the running of the company but these people will be employees, not owners.
- The partners in a partnership are usually all involved in the running of the business, although there are exceptions.
- In a limited company, the common position is for a board of directors to run the company on behalf of all owners, although all owners are allowed to vote for the board of directors at the Annual General Meeting.

Healthy Heaven has floated on the stock market – and you are a major shareholder. You have been elected onto the board of directors and have been asked by your fellow directors to prepare a presentation on the future direction of the company. Your presentation will be delivered at the Annual General Meeting of the company.

You are aware that there are other companies offering a similar kind of product in the area so you have decided that you have to come up with a **unique selling point (USP)**, which will set Healthy Heaven plc apart from the competition. You have also decided that Healthy Heaven plc should set up in other cities in Scotland. Assume Healthy Heaven plc originated in the nearest city to your home, so don't choose that city. **Choose another Scottish city**.

To sum up, your presentation should consist of:

- A new idea to make Healthy Heaven plc even more attractive to customers and set it apart from the competition. State why you think this idea would work.
- A recommended city and some background on that city with reasons for your choice.

Note: It may be that two directors have been asked to work on this together.

MAKE THE LINK

- We learn about the benefits of locating to a particular place in **Geography**.
- We learn about the process of voting in **Modern Studies**.

ACTIVITIES

TASK 1

Shareholders can vote to replace a board of directors if they disapprove of the way the company is being run. Suggest three reasons why shareholders may disapprove of the way in which the board of directors run the company.

TASK 2

If a limited company wants to expand, it can issue more shares in the company. This is called 'equity'. However, we must remember that the more shares that are issued, the more dividends will have to be paid out to shareholders from the profit made by the company. Suggest alternative ways of raising finance, including advantages and disadvantages of your suggestions. This could be set out in the form of a table with the headings **Type of finance, Advantages** and **Disadvantages**.

TASK 3

You have now decided on a date for the opening of Healthy Heaven plc in the new city. You are going to advertise the opening on local radio. With a partner, prepare a script to be used in the advert. If you have the necessary equipment, you could record the advert.

MY LEARNING CHECKLIST

Put a tick in the column to show how you think you got on with each statement.
Green means you got on really well with your learning in this area.
Amber means you did well with your learning.
Red means you need to do a bit of work on your learning.

	Good to go!	Getting there	Help needed
1. I understand the difference between ownership and control.			
2. I understand why some companies need a board of directors.			
3. I understand that limited companies hold Annual General Meetings to inform shareholders of what is happening in the company.			
4. I understand that companies need a unique selling point to get ahead of their competitors.			
5. I understand that firms need a source of finance in order to expand and improve.			

STAKEHOLDERS

A worker in an organisation could be said to be a stakeholder in that organisation. Without the organisation, the worker would have no job and therefore no way of making a living. Clearly, then, the worker is very much affected by the organisation.

However, every organisation has other stakeholders. Other groups, not just workers, are affected by organisations. Consider the following stakeholders in Tesco.

TOP TIP

A person can be a stakeholder on more than one count. For example, quite often a local resident affected by an organisation will also be an employee of that organisation.

EXAMPLE

My name is Brian Cole. I work in Tesco as a technical support adviser. I enjoy my job and am paid quite well. As well as my wage, I am allowed a staff discount on items purchased in Tesco. The existence of Tesco certainly affects me and that makes me a stakeholder in the company. As I am an employee of Tesco, I am an **internal** stakeholder.

My name is Mary Lindsay. I live near to Tesco. Before the supermarket was built, the roads in my area were quiet but now there is a lot of traffic and noise. I know that Tesco has brought much-needed jobs to the area but it has also brought unwanted changes. I have written to Tesco expressing my concerns. The fact that Tesco affects me makes me a stakeholder in the company. However, as I am not part of the company, I am an **external** stakeholder.

ACTIVITIES

TASK 1

The two examples of stakeholders given on page 36 are by no means the only examples. There are other examples of stakeholders. Some are shown in the list below. For each stakeholder, state whether you think it is internal (part of the organisation) or an external stakeholder (affected by the organisation but not part of it).

1. Managers who run the organisation
2. Owners of the organisation
3. Suppliers of goods and services to the organisation
4. The government
5. Customers or users of the organisation
6. Pressure groups, such as Greenpeace.

Compare your list with a partner's. Do you agree? If not, discuss your opinions to see if you can agree.

TASK 2

Look again at the list of stakeholders. Working with a partner, ask each other in turn why you believe each group to be stakeholders.

Write down your partner's responses and consider whether or not you agree.

TASK 3

Sometimes stakeholders can take action to influence what an organisation does or does not do. For example, Mary Lindsay wrote a letter to Tesco expressing her concerns about what was happening in her area. Consider again the list of stakeholders. With a partner, choose an organisation. Discuss with your partner what each stakeholder group could do to influence the organisation. One or both of you should jot down your thoughts. This may be used in class discussion later.

Remember, a stakeholder group can be part of any organisation in any sector of our economy. For example, you may choose an organisation in the voluntary sector.

MAKE THE LINK

- In **Geography** we learn why certain organisations choose to locate in a particular area.
- In **English**, we learn to write in a way which would be suitable for formal letters.

DID YOU KNOW?

It is much easier for an organisation to get permission to build on a piece of land which has already been built on. This is known as a 'brownfield site'. 'Greenfield sites' are sites which have never had buildings on them before. Planning permission to build on such sites is much more difficult to secure.

OUR EVERYDAY LIVES

People tend to be quite negative about a large building appearing in an area. However, there can be positive effects. For example, a derelict piece of land may be redeveloped, making it much more attractive. Can you think of any other positive effects that could be gained for an area? You could turn your ideas into a presentation.

INTERDISCIPLINARY PROJECT

STAKEHOLDERS

Often people have different points of view. For example your neighbour's trees may be spoiling your outlook. Your neighbour may want the trees for privacy in his garden but his trees affect you negatively. People who are affected by an organisation are stakeholders. They are affected in different ways (positively or negatively) by what the organisation does.

EXAMPLE

The Moonset Function Suite is owned and run by John Wells. John has applied for a licence so that functions in the premises can carry on later into the evening and early hours of the morning. Eleanor McLean, a tenant in a nearby residential block, objects to this plan and will write to John to make her feelings known. John knows he is likely to receive objections but feels confident that he can convince any objector that his plan is a good one.

Ronan Atkins is a hospitality student at Greenfield College and has heard about the plan for the Moonset to stay open late. He is hoping to get a job preparing finger food for buffets. Ronan lives locally so would have no problem getting home late.

Divide into groups of three. Take on a role as John, Eleanor or Ronan.

John's tasks	Eleanor's tasks	Ronan's tasks
1. Create a script for an advert on local radio which will go ahead if consent is given for late opening.	1. Write a letter to John Wells setting out your concerns if his plan goes ahead. Give your letter to John so that he can write a reply.	1. Write a letter to John Wells asking to be considered for a job preparing buffet food for functions.
2. Write a letter of reply to Eleanor explaining why you believe the plan will be good for the area.	2. Do some research to find out the name, address and other contact details for a local councillor whose support you could ask for. Note: you may have more than one councillor.	2. Make a list of suitable finger foods that you would include in the buffet menu to be sent with your letter to John.

MAKE THE LINK

- We learn about elected members and the process of electing them in **Modern Studies**.

ACTIVITIES

TASK 1

John Wells has decided to offer the function suite free of charge four times per month to local charitable organisations and not-for-profit clubs.

1. Suggest which days/times John should offer the function suite free and why these would be good times.
2. Suggest why John has decided to offer the function suite free.

TASK 2

Apart from the three stakeholders already discussed, suggest other stakeholder groups in the Moonset. These can be internal or external. State whether each stakeholder group is internal or external and what influence they could have on the Moonset.

TASK 3

John Wells is introducing a Teen Disco Rocks event between 5.00 p.m. and 7.00 p.m. on Friday evenings. John is doing this for the benefit of local kids and does not wish to make a profit on the event. However, he wants to cover costs. He estimates his costs to be: DJ £95, drinks and snacks £50, doormen £60, cleaner £20, cost of producing tickets £5. John would also like to keep aside £30 in case of any breakages. John believes all 130 tickets will sell.

Showing your working, calculate the cost of a ticket.

MY LEARNING CHECKLIST

Put a tick in the column to show how you think you got on with each statement.
Green means you got on really well with your learning in this area.
Amber means you did well with your learning.
Red means you need to do a bit of work on your learning.

	Good to go!	Getting there	Help needed
1. *I understand what makes a person a stakeholder in an organisation.*	○	○	○
2. *I understand that stakeholders can be affected both positively and negatively by organisations.*	○	○	○
3. *I understand that stakeholders can take action if they object to what an organisation is doing.*	○	○	○
4. *I understand how the cost of a product is calculated.*	○	○	○
5. *I know that private organisations sometimes exercise social responsibility by providing facilities for local people.*	○	○	○

DECISIONS, DECISIONS!

We all make decisions every day, from the small and seemingly insignificant, to large, possibly life-changing decisions. Just like people, organisations must make decisions too. Getting a decision wrong can have an effect on the success of the organisation, and the various groups of people associated with the organisation (stakeholders) will feel the impact.

In business language, decisions are put into three categories:

- A **strategic** decision tends to be a decision made by a **senior manager**, about something that will happen over a **long time span**, probably about five years.
- A **tactical** decision, made by **middle managers**, will help bring about the strategic decision. **The time span will be shorter**, probably about twelve months.
- An **operational** decision is made **daily** by **supervisors** to keep the organisation running smoothly.

EXAMPLE

Simply Food is part of Marks & Spencer. Food from M&S is regarded as being quite special and a bit of a treat. However, it became increasingly clear that fewer people could afford to buy food at the prices charged, in the present economic conditions. The M&S management decided it was time to make Simply Food attractive to more consumers.

It was decided that only having Simply Food inside M&S department stores was not a good idea. A decision was taken to have Simply Food outlets in locations away from stores, such as in railway stations. In addition, Simply Food started to appear in BP petrol stations, making it accessible to many more consumers. It was also decided to start selling a cheaper range called 'Wise Buys'. Also, branded items, such as Heinz, started to appear – previously unheard of in M&S.

Such change may well have helped M&S through the difficult economic conditions but store managers would also have had to play their part in keeping Simply Food popular. Keeping stores well stocked and in good order, and training staff up to a good standard are all just as important as decisions made by more senior managers.

TOP TIP

We should all use the time available to us when making decisions. Rushing into a decision without due consideration can lead to a poor decision being made. A response is usually better than a reaction. Perhaps you could take the time to consider the meanings of these two words. Why might a response be better than a reaction?

ACTIVITIES

TASK 1

Make a list of all the decisions mentioned in the passage about Simply Food. Once you have your list, compare it with your partner's. Do you have all the same decisions? Once you have agreed on a full list, decide if the decisions are strategic, tactical or operational.

TASK 2

Look at the following examples of decisions. Are they strategic, tactical or operational?

1. To have all staff in the organisation highly trained in customer service.
2. To book places on training courses for all managers.
3. To ensure that all staff in departments carry out good customer service.
4. To introduce self-service checkouts to 80% of stores within five years.
5. To decide on the first 20% of stores to have self-service brought in during year one.
6. To train staff in stores to supervise the self-service checkouts.

TASK 3

Information is very useful to help make decisions. The managers of M&S may well have collected market research to help them decide what to do. For example, one question might have been:

Where would you like to see Simply Food outlets located?

The answers might have included: railway stations, petrol stations.

Write down two or three more questions likely to have been asked in the research and the likely answers.

MAKE THE LINK

- In **Social Education**, we learn how to make good personal decisions.
- In **Maths**, we learn how percentages are calculated.
- In **English**, we learn about words and their meanings.

DID YOU KNOW?

The Scottish Government decided to change the law to make it illegal to buy alcohol in Scottish stores before 10 o'clock in the morning. This is to try to reduce consumption of alcohol for the sake of the health and well-being of the country.

OUR EVERYDAY LIVES

The management of M&S decided to charge customers for plastic carrier bags to try to encourage the reuse of bags. On the other hand, Tesco award points for bag reuse. Which do you think will be more effective? You could discuss this in class.

TASK 4

A company has fifty stores and decides that:

1. 20% of stores will have self-service checkouts by the end of year one. How many stores will have self-service checkouts by the end of year one?
2. 80% of stores will have self-service checkouts by the end of year five. How many stores will have self-service checkouts by the end of year five?
3. In the first store to have self-service checkouts introduced, fifteen out of sixty staff will be trained to supervise the self-service checkouts. Calculate this as a percentage.

INTERDISCIPLINARY PROJECT

DECISIONS, DECISIONS!

Middle managers make tactical decisions, which help to drive through decisions made by senior managers. The strategic decisions put in place by senior managers will not succeed if they are not supported well by the tactical decision-makers.

You and a partner have been employed by John Wells of the Moonset Function Suite, as middle managers directly responsible to John. John's strategic decision is to increase his profits by 5–10% in the next three years. With your partner, you are going to prepare a tactical plan, which will ensure John will achieve his increase in profits. Your plan will only include new events that will help achieve the profit increase. Think about maximising the usage of the Moonset, not just in the evenings. It might be an idea to draw up a schedule of days and evenings with possible events for the various time slots.

You may be asked to present your plan to the rest of your class.

MAKE THE LINK

- Two skills that are vital in all of our subjects are **decision-making** and **communicating**.

ACTIVITIES

TASK 1

Good decisions are based on information, which often comes from research.

1. Suggest how research could be carried out to find out which events would be popular at the Moonset.
2. Suggest possible consequences of not carrying out research.

TASK 2

John may employ supervisors to ensure day-to-day tasks are carried out well. One such task is preparing a staff rota.

1. Suggest problems which could occur as a result of under-staffing or employing staff who are not appropriately trained to carry out tasks.
2. State why over-staffing may also be damaging for a business like the Moonset Function Suite.

TASK 3

Look at the following decisions and state whether you think they are strategic, tactical or operational.

1. Open up more branches around the UK over the next five years.
2. Order stock of stationery.
3. Decide on appropriate premises to be rented for new branch.
4. Decide on a firm of decorators to paint the new branches.
5. Arrange for uplift of waste for recycling.

TASK 4

It is essential that decision-makers on different levels communicate well so that they work together for the ultimate good of the organisation.

- Suggest suitable ways in which all decision-makers in a business can communicate.
- State why you would recommend these ways of communicating.

MY LEARNING CHECKLIST

Put a tick in the column to show how you think you got on with each statement.
Green means you got on really well with your learning in this area.
Amber means you did well with your learning.
Red means you need to do a bit of work on your learning.

	Good to go!	Getting there	Help needed
1. I understand that decisions are made at different levels in organisations.	○	○	○
2. I understand that different levels of decision-making have different time spans.	○	○	○
3. I understand good decision-making is based on good information.	○	○	○
4. I understand the consequences of poor decision-making in organisations.	○	○	○
5. I understand the importance of effective communication between decision-makers.	○	○	○

WHAT AFFECTS A BUSINESS?

No matter how effective a business is, how hard its employees work or how well its products sell, what happens in the outside **environment** will also affect the business. For example, the recent difficulties in our economy have resulted in businesses getting into trouble or even failing altogether. Another example is the heavy snow in December 2010 which meant Christmas sales in shops suffered.

Similarly, changes in the law can affect businesses. If, for example, the law changed so that the lowest hourly rate of pay went up to £10 per hour, this could have a real impact on businesses who might find it difficult to pay their employees at this rate.

TOP TIP

UK holidaymakers are increasingly enthusiastic about all-inclusive holidays. The cost of the holiday may be higher than other package holidays to Mediterranean destinations but less spending money is required because all drinks and food consumed in the hotel are free. All-inclusive has become particularly popular during the period when the British pound has been weak against the euro.

EXAMPLE

Harry Hislop and his wife, Betty, have run Hislop's Coach Tours since 1995. Since they started trading, Harry and Betty have seen the value of the British pound rise and fall. This is particularly important to Harry and Betty as the majority of their customers are from mainland Europe and the USA. Harry and Betty see a very noticeable fall in bookings when the British pound is strong because their customers have to use more of their currency to buy pounds to pay for Harry and Betty's service. However, a weak pound also affects the business. A weak pound makes it more expensive to buy fuel from overseas which, in turn, makes it more expensive to run the coach.

ACTIVITIES

TASK 1

The following prices are taken from the current brochure for Hislop's Coach Tours. The prices are in British pounds but a French customer and an American customer have each asked that the prices be given in their own currencies.

Find out the current value of £1 in (a) euros and (b) US dollars.

Convert each of the prices into that currency.

If you are not able to find out the exchange rates, use the following information:
£1 = €1·15
£1 = $1·57
Present your answers in a table.

Tour	Month	Price in sterling	Price in euros	Price in US dollars
Highland Magic 7-day tour	April	Adult price £350		
Highland Magic 7-day tour	April	Child price £250		
Borders Beauty 10-day tour	June	Adult price £540		
Borders Beauty 10-day tour	June	Child price £310		

TASK 2

Some changes to the law could affect Hislop's Coach Tours. Suggest how the following changes would affect the business.

1. The rest breaks a coach driver must take become longer and more frequent.
2. All coaches must have toilet and wash facilities.
3. The speed limit for coaches is reduced.

MAKE THE LINK

- In **Modern Studies**, we learn how laws protect citizens.
- In **Geography**, we learn about imports and exports from other countries.
- In **Social Education**, we learn about road safety.
- In **Maths**, we learn how to perform calculations.

DID YOU KNOW?

Coach drivers must by law take a rest of forty-five minutes after driving for four hours and thirty minutes. This is because driver fatigue is a significant cause of traffic accidents. If there is time, discuss with a partner other factors which cause traffic accidents.

OUR EVERYDAY LIVES

Laws control all of our lives. These may be local by-laws put in place by our local council, laws made in Edinburgh by the Scottish Parliament, by the UK Parliament in London or even by the European Parliament in Brussels. Perhaps you could find out about a recent law which has been passed through the Scottish Parliament.

TASK 3

Another outside influence which can affect a business is **competition**. Another business fighting for the same customers will have a considerable impact. Imagine you are a competitor of Hislop's Coach Tours. Create a presentation detailing what you would offer. Include:

- the name of your tour company
- where your tours go to
- any special deals you plan to offer, for example discounts
- anything else you think will attract customers.

INTERDISCIPLINARY PROJECT

WHAT AFFECTS A BUSINESS?

The quality of decision-making in an organisation will affect its success. However, other factors – beyond the control of the organisation – can also make a positive or negative difference to the organisation. These are known as 'external influences'. That does not mean that the business cannot take steps to protect itself from, or indeed take advantage of, the influence.

With a partner, write a case study about a business. Choose a small business that can either be fictional or based on a real business.

You will have to:

- agree on what should be included in the case study
- divide the writing fairly
- write on separate pages.

The business in your case study should be affected by the following external influences:

- a new law or a change to an existing law, such as an increase in the minimum wage
- exceptional weather
- a sudden rise or fall in the popularity of the company's product and a reason for that change in popularity
- a competing business setting up nearby.

Once the class has completed the case studies, each pair should read theirs aloud. Each pair in the class may be awarded the following marks:

1 mark for including each of the four external factors and **3** marks for the quality of the case study, taking into account the level of interest in the case study. The maximum mark is therefore **7**.

MAKE THE LINK

- We learn about the impact of crime on our society in **Modern Studies** and **Social Education**.

ACTIVITIES

TASK 1

The case study you have written should be typed up and formatted to look attractive on the page. You may be able to use Microsoft Publisher for this task. Each partner should key in half of the case study. Improve the look of the document with the use of images, a page border and Word Art. The case study (on two pages) would make a good wall display.

TASK 2

One major external factor affecting organisations is crime. Discuss with your partner the kind of crime that could affect the organisation in your case study. You could make this into a presentation.

TASK 3

Look at the following influences affecting a department store and state whether you think they are internal or external:

1. A fire broke out in the stockroom.
2. The price of visitor parking in a neighbouring council-run car park has increased by 20%.
3. The rate of inflation rose, leading to a general rise in prices.
4. There was a rise in customer complaints due to poor customer service.
5. There was an upward trend in online shopping.

TASK 4

Apart from crime, make a list of external influences that an organisation could insure against.

MY LEARNING CHECKLIST

Put a tick in the column to show how you think you got on with each statement.
Green means you got on really well with your learning in this area.
Amber means you did well with your learning.
Red means you need to do a bit of work on your learning.

		Good to go!	Getting there	Help needed
1.	*I understand that factors influencing organisations can be internal or external.*	◯	◯	◯
2.	*I understand that organisations can take steps to protect themselves against internal and external factors.*	◯	◯	◯
3.	*I understand the impact of crime on organisations.*	◯	◯	◯
4.	*I understand that changes in technology have had a big impact on organisations.*	◯	◯	◯
5.	*I understand that during a recession some businesses will find it difficult to survive.*	◯	◯	◯

COMPUTERS – WHAT'S GOING ON INSIDE?

Most of us use computers and many of us use them every day. Although we can't see what's going on inside the computer, there are applications (or software) inside that make the computer operate.

There are lots of different software packages available to buy. A particular organisation may well require a certain type of software for the kind of work they do. However, three very commonly used types of software package are:

- spreadsheet
- database
- word-processing.

You may be familiar with these types of software package if brand names are used. Microsoft is a popular brand. Under the name of Microsoft Office, it provides a spreadsheet package called Excel, a database package called Access and word-processing package called Word.

EXAMPLE

Invite Me! is a small company in Edinburgh. It designs personalised invitations and acceptances for all sorts of events. These products are different from more conventional products offered by competing companies. This makes these products popular among a relatively small group of consumers – 'a niche market'.

Invite Me! uses Microsoft Office products. It uses Excel for calculating how much it is owed by clients. Contact details of suppliers of card and other materials are all kept in an Access database. Invite Me! sends letters to clients and other stakeholders; these are word-processed using Word. While Excel, Access and Word are used by very many organisations, perhaps fewer use Microsoft Publisher, which is a desktop publishing package. This package is used by Invite Me! specifically for creating their products.

TOP TIP

A cell in a spreadsheet can be changed so that its contents appear in a particular way, such as a date or currency. This is called "formatting".

ACTIVITIES

TASK 1

The image shows an extract from a spreadsheet used by Invite Me! It shows clients who are yet to pay what they owe. A formula could be keyed into cell D10 to add all of the amounts owed. A label could be keyed into cell C10 to identify the **total owed**.

◇	A	B	C	D
1	**Client title**	**Client initial**	**Client last name**	**Outstanding amount**
2	Mrs	F	Gorden	£ 269·21
3	Mr	G	Henry	£ 127·92
4	Miss	D	Anderson	£ 143·98
5	Mr	T	Lomond	£ 277·11
6	Mrs	A	Smith	£ 209·55
7	Mr	D	Gorden	£ 232·87
8	Mrs	R	Green	£ 189·45
9	Miss	J	Ross	£ 143·98

If you have access to a computer, you could key this data into a spreadsheet. Alternatively, write down the formula which would be keyed into cell D10.

TASK 2

The data used in the spreadsheet could also be contained in a database. If you are able to use a computer, you could key the data into a database. You could put another field into the database with the title: Client number. Give each client a number starting at 1.

- Sort the data by client number.
- Filter the database so that only those with the title Mr are shown.
- State why you think the database needs unique client numbers.

TASK 3

Design a letterhead for Invite Me! which would appear on its stationery. Make the letterhead suitable for a company of this type. Include these contact details. Address: 14 High Street, Edinburgh EH1 2TT. Telephone: 0131 555 7712. Website: www.inviteme.co.uk. Include a logo.

MAKE THE LINK

- In **English**, we learn how to use language in an appropriate way.
- In **Maths**, we learn how to add numbers with or without the aid of spreadsheets or calculators.
- In **Art and Design**, we learn how to design logos.

DID YOU KNOW?

The obvious benefits of using computer software are the time it saves and the reduction in errors being made. However, it is also useful for security because a computer protected with a password will protect data which may be confidential. Another benefit is the space that can be saved. Keeping paper records stored in filing cabinets is very space-consuming. Information kept electronically is much more space-efficient, as a great deal can be saved on the computer's hard drive or indeed on another storage device. If you have time, you could come up with a list of devices for storing data electronically. You could set a time limit and race a partner. Who thought of the most in the time allowed?

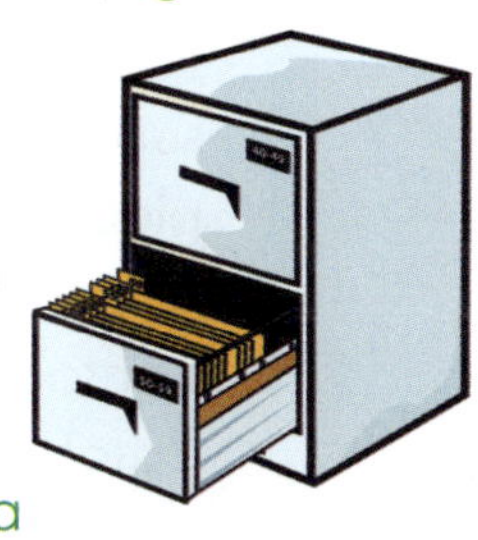

OUR EVERYDAY LIVES

We may put off paying a bill, but this can be bad news for a company. Failure to get their clients or customers to pay on time can lead to the company being unable to pay their bills. This can cause the company to fail.

INTERDISCIPLINARY PROJECT

COMPUTERS – WHAT'S GOING ON INSIDE?

A business such as the Moonset Function Suite would benefit from software packages.

- Fewer errors are made or they are easily corrected.
- The packages save time compared to performing the tasks manually.
- The finish is slick and professional, which is much more impressive.

You have been asked to perform tasks using a computer for the Moonset Function Suite:

1. Using a spreadsheet, key in the details of costs for the Teen Disco Rocks event. Use the information given on page 39. Lay out the information as follows:
   The shaded cells should contain formulae and the five cells above the shaded cells should contain values. Format cells for currency as appropriate.

◇	A	B
1	**Cost**	**Amount**
2	DJ	
3	Drinks and snacks	
4	Doormen	
5	Cleaner	
6	Cost of producing tickets	
7	**Total**	
8	Number of tickets sold	
9	Tickets price	

2. A database record is a set of information about, for example, a company's suppliers. A field is a single piece of information from a record, for example, a contact name. Using a database, key in the records and fields as follows:
   - The date for the first three supplier orders is today's date. The others are yesterday's date.
   - Sort the database by **last order date** (most recent first) and **supplier name**.

Supplier name	Contact name	Last order date
JL Supplies	Sally	
Gr8 Snax	Thomas	
Lord & Co.	Austin	
Sweets 4U	Claire	
C Glass Ltd	Angie	

MAKE THE LINK

- In RME we learn about organisations donating to the communities in which they exist.

ACTIVITIES

TASK 1

John Wells is considering setting up a website for the business.

1. Make a list of content you would recommend for John's website.
2. State reasons why you believe the Moonset would benefit from having a website.

TASK 2

John originally decided to run the disco with no profit and was happy just to cover his costs.

1. Using the spreadsheet, calculate the ticket price if John now decides he wants to make a profit of £65.
2. Again using the spreadsheet, calculate the ticket price if John decides he wants to make a profit of £195.

TASK 3

With a partner, discuss the benefits likely to be gained by an organisation using:

1. A spreadsheet
2. A database
3. Word-processing

Now write down your thoughts, which could be made into a poster or presentation.

TASK 4

Discuss with a partner the costs likely to be felt by an organisation of introducing technology. Again, write down your thoughts, which could be used later in a poster or presentation.

MY LEARNING CHECKLIST

Put a tick in the column to show how you think you got on with each statement.
Green means you got on really well with your learning in this area.
Amber means you did well with your learning.
Red means you need to do a bit of work on your learning.

	Good to go!	Getting there	Help needed
1. ***I understand that calculations can be performed using spreadsheets.***	○	○	○
2. ***I understand the difference between a field and a record in a database.***	○	○	○
3. ***I understand the benefit of using word-processing.***	○	○	○
4. ***I understand that organisations benefit from having websites.***	○	○	○
5. ***I understand that there are costs and benefits of introducing technology into an organisation.***	○	○	○

INFORMATION

It would be difficult, if not impossible, to run any kind of organisation without information. Every **stakeholder** in an organisation will require some kind of information. An example of a stakeholder in an organisation is an **employee**. An employee may be very interested to know how profitable an organisation has been in the last year before getting into talks about pay rises.

An external stakeholder, such as a **local resident**, may want to know how large a proposed new building for an organisation is likely to be. They may make an objection to the council if they are unhappy about the size of the building.

Nowadays, we have a great deal of access to a great deal of information. The best example of this is the internet. We can access useful information simply by putting some key terms into a search engine such as Google. However, we can be overwhelmed by the volume of information available, and we have no guarantee about the accuracy of what we read.

EXAMPLE

When Philip Moore first thought about starting a business selling fast food to go, he used the internet to do some research to find out about similar businesses in the area. He also did research on foot, delivering questionnaires to local addresses in the hope that at least some locals would reply with their thoughts on the likely success of such a venture. Once Philip decided to go ahead with his business, he used the local newspaper to find premises suitable to rent. He also used the internet again to find out what he would have to do to get permission to sell hot food from his premises.

TOP TIP

When information is collected for a particular reason, we call this **primary** information. An example of this is a survey designed to find out what people think about school uniform. On the other hand, information can be **secondary**. It may be that the information was previously collected for another purpose and is being used again. An example of this would be a newspaper article about opinions on school uniform.

ACTIVITIES

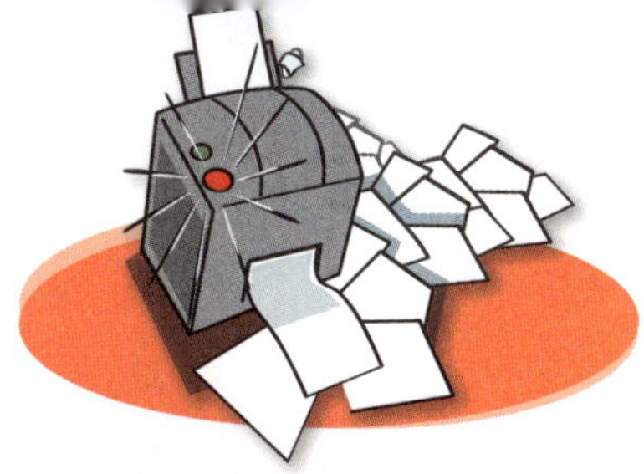

TASK 1

Identify the examples of information Philip found. State whether or not the information was found electronically. Display your findings in a table.

TASK 2

Discuss with a partner the ways used by Philip to find information. Between you, come up with at least **two** advantages and two disadvantages of finding information electronically.

TASK 3

Now that Philip has premises and permission to sell hot food, suggest other information that will be useful for him to start trading. You should work with a partner. Between you, come up with a list of good ideas about information he will need and why he will need it. You may wish to make this into a presentation.

TASK 4

The examples of information used by Philip are all **external** because he found the information outside of his organisation. He may over time build up information inside his business which may be useful in the future. For example, he will probably keep information regarding profit (or loss) made.

1. Suggest why past profits might be useful information for Philip in the future.
2. Suggest another internal stakeholder who might be interested in Philip's profits.
3. Suggest an external stakeholder who might be interested in Philip's profits.
4. Suggest some other examples of internal information which Philip might have in his business.

MAKE THE LINK

- In **Modern Studies**, we learn about laws and how they affect organisations.
- In **Maths**, we learn how profits are calculated.
- In **Home Economics**, we learn about requirements for food preparation and about what goes into the food we eat.

DID YOU KNOW?

More and more restaurants and takeaways are now stating clearly the fat, sugar and calorie contents of what they sell. This is popular with many customers because it saves confusion. For example, a salad or sandwich may be less healthy than first thought because of the high fat and calorie content of its dressing.

OUR EVERYDAY LIVES

Preparing and storing food is a very serious business. It is not unknown for people to become unwell, or even die, because laws and guidelines have not been followed correctly with regard to food preparation and storage. Businesses selling food are regularly inspected and can be closed down if procedures have not been properly followed. You could carry out some research yourself to find out what is required with regard to preparing and serving food.

INTERDISCIPLINARY PROJECT

INFORMATION

In organisations, information is crucial for decision-making. It is important to know where to access the information we need. The internet is very useful but it is easy to forget that often the accuracy of what appears online goes unchecked. We cannot always rely on information found online.

Using information found online, or another source, find contact details for a prominent local person, such as your Member of the Scottish Parliament (MSP), your Member of Parliament (MP) or a local councillor. It would be interesting to find out about how an elected member serves your community. Equally, your choice of local person could be a local businessperson or a minister, priest, rabbi or other minister of religion. Check your choice with your teacher so that the person only receives one letter from your class.

With your partner, decide on what you would like to ask the person. Once this has been decided, you should neatly write or type your letter. Decide between you who should write or type up the letter. Perhaps you could both contribute.

When your letter has been checked and approved by your teacher, it can be posted. In time, it would be good to create a display of replies received. When you receive a reply, it is good practice to write again to thank the prominent person for taking the time to write to you.

MAKE THE LINK

- In **Social Education** and in **Modern Studies**, we learn about the way we, as consumers, are protected by laws.

ACTIVITIES

TASK 1

You have written a letter to seek out information. Write down any advantages or disadvantages of using a letter to gather information.

TASK 2

John Wells of Moonset Function Suite has decided to order stocks of crisps and nuts from Gr8 Snax. However, John has used a price list issued by Gr8 Snax a year ago to find out the price of the items being purchased.

1. Suggest consequences for John of using the out-of-date price list.
2. Suggest why using an online price list might have been more reliable.

TASK 3

1. John went online and read that JL Supplies have a special offer this month of 20% off orders over £50. John's order amounted to £87. Calculate the amount John would expect to pay. Show your workings.
2. John was disappointed to find that the information online was not clear and, in fact, the 20% discount is only on the part of the order over £50.
   Again showing your workings, recalculate the amount John will have to pay.

TASK 4

Discuss with a partner the likely consequences of unclear or misleading information being passed to customers.

MY LEARNING CHECKLIST

Put a tick in the column to show how you think you got on with each statement.
Green means you got on really well with your learning in this area.
Amber means you did well with your learning.
Red means you need to do a bit of work on your learning.

	Good to go!	Getting there	Help needed
1. ***I understand that information found online is not necessarily reliable.***	◯	◯	◯
2. ***I understand that an elected member is chosen by voters to represent them.***	◯	◯	◯
3. ***I understand the importance of reading information carefully to ensure the message has been properly understood.***	◯	◯	◯
4. ***I understand that there are many sources of information, both paper-based and electronic.***	◯	◯	◯
5. ***I understand how a percentage discount is calculated.***	◯	◯	◯

OUR ELECTRONIC AGE

Some would say that the lives we live nowadays are much improved by our access to technology. Most would agree that technology has made our lives more convenient. Perhaps we take this convenience for granted. Some people believe that our way of life was better before our electronic age.

Not so long ago, almost all of our shopping was done by going to stores, choosing items and buying them. Other methods of buying did exist, such as ordering from a catalogue. However, buying from high street stores or shopping centres (retail outlets) dominated our shopping habits. How times have changed.

Towards the end of 2010, it was estimated that, on 6 December, £23 million per hour would be spent on internet shopping in the UK alone. Retailers are aware of the ever-growing popularity of this way of shopping – and have responded by giving consumers what they want.

TOP TIP
Businesses should be careful not to overlook customers who do not shop online. It is estimated that between 9 and 10 million people in the UK have no internet access so a business ignoring that group of people could be missing out on a lot of sales.

EXAMPLE

Jayne Harman has a disability which makes it difficult for her to leave home unaided. However, Jayne is able to live alone and is very independent.

Up until a few years ago, Jayne had to rely on a friend taking her shopping or bringing her shopping to her. Nowadays, Jayne does a lot of her shopping online as many of the shops she uses provide this facility, together with a delivery service. This does not, however, mean that Jayne does all of her shopping online. She still enjoys shopping trips with friends, much like anyone else. Nonetheless, Jayne does find online shopping useful and many others agree. The growth in internet sales would confirm this.

ACTIVITIES

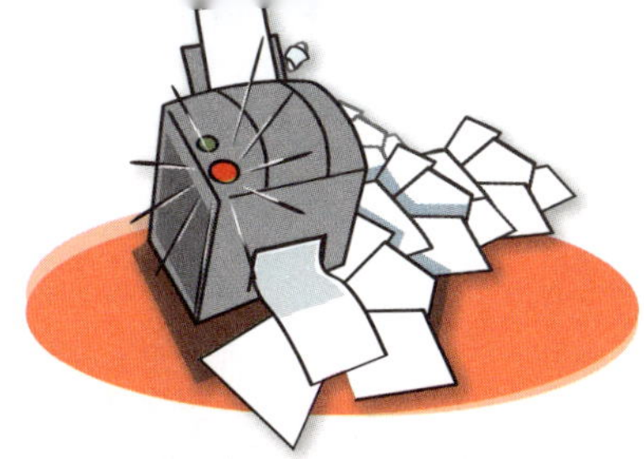

TASK 1

Amazon.com is a popular online retailer which was founded in 1995. It began by selling books but now sells many more products, from toys and games to power tools.

Answer the following questions:

1. Suggest why Amazon now sells a wider range of products.
2. As a consumer, why might you choose to shop at Amazon rather than a high street store?
3. Amazon also sell clothes. You have decided to buy an item of clothing for a special occasion in the near future. Why might you decide against buying the item from Amazon?
4. Suggest an online retailer well known for selling (a) low cost air travel; (b) car insurance.

TASK 2

Design a home page for an online retailer. You may consider an online seller of sportswear or you may wish to choose one of your own. Make sure you have a suitable name and logo for your online retailer. Your home page should be attractive and include an introduction with details of the products sold, a delivery pledge and a returns policy.

Your home page should include links to other pages. It may help to look online at other sites to get ideas for web pages and the layout of your home page. You could work with a partner on this task.

TASK 3

Tesco is just one example of a business providing online shopping with home delivery. Discuss with a partner:

1. why Tesco (or another business providing a similar service) chooses to provide this service for customers
2. any problems that might affect this service.

MAKE THE LINK

- In **Art and Design**, we create designs which could be used for a business logo.
- In **Maths**, we learn how percentages are calculated.

DID YOU KNOW?

At one time, consumers may have been discouraged from ordering goods and receiving them by post because the item might be damaged in transit. The Jiffy Bag has gone a long way towards solving this problem. A simple brown envelope (of various sizes) lined with bubble wrap is ideal protection for a variety of products in the post. In addition, the Jiffy Bag can be reused for posting items in the future.

OUR EVERYDAY LIVES

There is very little nowadays that cannot be purchased online. This is a big benefit to people who cannot leave home, such as people housebound because of ill-health and the elderly. However, our pace of life in the second decade of the new millennium means that being able to order Christmas gifts, or even the weekly food shop, online is a big help.

TASK 4

It is quite usual for online traders to charge for delivery. For example, myShop.com charges £3 for weekday delivery within four days, £5 for 24-hour weekday delivery and £6 for delivery on a Saturday. Jayne Harman purchased a skirt costing £30 from myShop.com. Calculate the percentage charged to Jayne for having her skirt delivered if she:

1. accepts weekday delivery within four days
2. accepts weekday 24-hour delivery
3. accepts Saturday delivery.

INTERDISCIPLINARY PROJECT

OUR ELECTRONIC AGE

What could be described as an 'electronic revolution' has changed our lives. Communication is at the heart of this revolution. Most of us own mobile phones and can be reached at any time. We can even send and receive emails from some phones.

Video conferencing has made a huge difference in business. This method of holding meetings in real time with a number of other people, possibly in locations around the world, has contributed to reducing costs. Although the technology is expensive, the savings made on travel and time away from the workplace are substantial. It also reduces our carbon footprint as fewer journeys are required. Some people believe that nothing compares to meeting another person 'in the flesh' and may criticise technology for failing at the very worst time. Nevertheless, many organisations use this technology.

You have recently joined a company called Link-IT. The company sells electronic communication products worldwide and in the near future will launch a video-conferencing system. The working name for the product is **in-the-room**.

With a partner, you have been asked to write a script for a one-minute launch advert. The advert will be shown exclusively as a pop-up online. You will have to:

- Write the script. Remember to be **informative** but at the same time you have to grab the attention of potential customers, so use language that sells the product.
- Edit the script. Remember your one-minute time slot. Be careful to keep in all the essential information.
- Record the script. If you have time, rehearse your script and listen back. Be critical of what you don't think works well.

Tip: Using two voices often helps to hold the attention of potential customers.

MAKE THE LINK

- In **English** and in **Drama**, we learn how to write scripts and choose appropriate language.

ACTIVITIES

TASK 1

The name **in-the-room** is a working title, which means that a different name may be chosen later. Can you think of a better name?

- With your partner, discuss the name **in-the-room**. Do you think the name will work for the product? Write down any reasons why you think it is a suitable name and also any criticisms you may have.
- Now come up with an alternative name. Remember what you are selling and the market you are selling the product to. Write down reasons for your choice. You may, of course, disagree on the name and will have to convince your partner about your choice.

TASK 2

In one minute, write down as many methods of electronic communication as you can think of. After one minute, compare your list with your partner's. Who won? Check each other's lists. Your partner may have written down a method more than once, or perhaps one or more methods are not actually electronic.

TASK 3

Link-IT has decided to advertise its new product online as a 'pop-up'. Write down any advantages and disadvantages of using this method of advertising.

TASK 4

More and more businesses are using texts as a method of communicating. Discuss with a partner ways in which a car repair business could use texts to improve communication. The result of your discussion could be made into a presentation.

MY LEARNING CHECKLIST

Put a tick in the column to show how you think you got on with each statement.
Green means you got on really well with your learning in this area.
Amber means you did well with your learning.
Red means you need to do a bit of work on your learning.

	Good to go!	Getting there	Help needed
1. *I understand that modern businesses use electronic methods of communicating.*	○	○	○
2. *I understand that online sales is a major growth area worldwide.*	○	○	○
3. *I understand that electronic communication can reduce our carbon footprint.*	○	○	○
4. *I understand the importance of using the right language in advertising.*	○	○	○
5. *I understand that getting the name of a product right can make a big difference to its success.*	○	○	○

TEAMWORK

When an organisation sets out to achieve something, we call this an 'objective' or 'goal'. This will be reached more easily if everyone involved works together. This will require planning and 'teamwork'.

We often hear the expression 'working as a team'. Indeed, many of us will play team sports such as football. Team players cooperate, which means they all help each other to reach a common goal. This is most likely to succeed if:

- The team members communicate well together so they are all agreed on their common goal and how to get there. They must also be prepared to listen to each other.
- The team has 'the right mix'. This doesn't necessarily mean they all should have the same views and opinions but they must be able to work well together.
- Team members have a variety of skills and talents. For example, one team member might be an ideas person, while another is good at putting the ideas into practice.
- The team is the right size for the task being carried out. If the task is quite straightforward, there may be no need to have an overly-large team.
- The task is clear. If what is to be achieved is unclear or confused, different team members may understand the objective differently, leading to real problems.

TOP TIP
When working as part of a team you should think about your own skills and talents. How can you best contribute to the overall success of the team? A good team member will not think about their individual success but rather the ultimate success of the team.

As important as the skills for teamwork are, it doesn't mean a different person is needed for each task. In fact, some individuals may be able to fulfil more than one task.

ACTIVITIES

TASK 1

A school is holding an inter-house competition which involves teams planning an afternoon tea event for senior citizens. The school will use the best plan and the winning house will receive a prize of a barbecue in the school garden.

Answer the following questions:

1. Why is it important for the teams to have ideas people?
2. Why might it be a problem if every team member was an ideas person?
3. Suggest roles for other team members in this competition.

TASK 2

In a team of three or four, come up with your own plan for the senior citizen tea. Consider factors such as the date, the venue, what food and drinks will be served and the entertainment.

TASK 3

Suggest a task that could be carried out successfully by a team in the following settings. (The first one has been done for you.)

Setting	Team task
NHS hospital	Drive to improve ward hygiene
Restaurant	
Supermarket	
Public library	

TASK 4

Working as a team can be of benefit – but things can go wrong. Make a list of factors which may stop the team from being successful. (The first one has been done for you.)

1. There may be too many team members who want to take on the same role.
2.
3.
4.
5.

MAKE THE LINK

- In most of our school subjects, we sometimes work in teams. This may be most obvious in **PE** where many team sports are played. However, in **Home Economics** we may make dishes which require teamwork. **Art and Design** is another good example.

DID YOU KNOW?

There is no doubt that working as a team will improve output. One important factor is that often a team member will not want to be seen as 'the weakest link', so will work harder to gain the respect and admiration of their team-mates.

Think of a time when you were part of a team. Did you work hard? What do you feel made you work hard?

OUR EVERYDAY LIVES

Going into hospital is an anxious time for anyone but it is an everyday reality for lots of people. The care offered to patients in hospitals up and down the country will not be carried out by one single medical person. In fact, there will be a team of people all playing a role in the care of a patient, from the doctor diagnosing the problem, to an occupational therapist helping the patient to gain back skills they may have lost during their period of illness.

INTERDISCIPLINARY PROJECT

TEAMWORK

We are all familiar with the word 'team'. For example, we know that a 'team sport', such as football, is a sport which requires team members to work together. Different team members will have different specialities, based on their skills and talents. However, the overall aim will be the same for every team member: to be as successful as possible. The same is true of teamwork in an organisation.

Invite Me! wants to develop an online version of its service. The idea is that users of its website key in details for their invitations and/or acceptances and Invite Me! provides the product electronically. The user would then either print the product or send it electronically.

Teamwork is important to this organisation and so a team is to be formed to carry out the project. It is considered important that all team members have roles based on what they are good at. The following team roles have been identified for the project:

Team leader 	Ensures that the operation is proceeding well and that all team members are cooperating with each other.
Troubleshooter 	Highlights difficulties and glitches in ideas which have been suggested – and fixes them.
Financial wizard 	Looks after all the financial issues connected with the project.
Resource magnet 	Sources all resources needed for the project, from drinks for team meetings to training needs for staff.

Which team role matches your skills set? Having read all four team roles, decide which one is right for you. Key in an email, to be sent to the operations manager, stating why you would be right for this team role. Include examples of occasions when you have demonstrated the necessary skills.

MAKE THE LINK

- Learning to work as a team is important in PE but, in fact, it is important in all subjects as we learn to work with others for the best possible outcome.

ACTIVITIES

TASK 1

You are part of a team in school, which has been asked to plan a farewell party for a friend who is leaving. Decide what will have to be done and who will take on each role. You have a budget of £100.

Come up with an action plan setting out tasks that have to be done and the order of tasks. Decide also who will carry out each task. The only conditions given are that you must provide:

- simple finger food for twenty people
- some kind of music and decorations.

TASK 2

You are a member of a youth group. A fund-raising project has been organised: the youth group will make Easter pots. This requires empty 1-litre ice-cream cartons to be covered in coloured tissue paper. Easter ribbon will be wrapped around each pot, and finally different coloured mini Easter eggs will be arranged attractively in the baskets. You have been put into teams of four and there will be a prize of cinema tickets for the team producing the highest number of top-quality pots.

- Devise an action plan, which will result in your team winning the tickets.
- State what you took into consideration when deciding on your action plan.

TASK 3

Task 2 involves planning a task. This task involves putting a plan into practice. Task 2 could be adapted for any season or occasion. For example, a tub covered in Christmas paper with tinsel wrapped around it would be great for Christmas presents, with sweets or nuts and oranges inside.

In your team, decide on the kind of pots you would like to make and how you should go about making them. It will be necessary to make a plan. You will also have to make sure you have all the materials you need. This could be carried out over lunch.

MY LEARNING CHECKLIST

Put a tick in the column to show how you think you got on with each statement.
Green means you got on really well with your learning in this area.
Amber means you did well with your learning.
Red means you need to do a bit of work on your learning.

	Good to go!	Getting there	Help needed
1. ***I understand that an organisation's success can be improved by effective teamwork.***	○	○	○
2. ***I understand that different people with the appropriate skills and talents can fulfil different team roles.***	○	○	○
3. ***I understand that disagreements and personality clashes can happen within teams.***	○	○	○
4. ***I understand that team objectives must be clear, otherwise there can be confusion among team members.***	○	○	○
5. ***I understand that a team will only be successful if each team member works for the good of the team, rather than for individual success.***	○	○	○

THE CULTURE OF AN ORGANISATION

Different organisations operate in different ways. Some organisations operate in a formal way, whereas others are more relaxed. In the past, the culture of an organisation has been described as: 'The way things get done around here.'

While one culture may work for one organisation, a different culture may work for another. It is, however, important that everyone working for that organisation understands, and works well within, the culture of that organisation.

TOP TIP
Adopting an organisation's culture does not necessarily mean losing your individuality. Organisations benefit from individual thought and inspiration. This may, in fact, add to the success of the culture of an organisation.

Some organisations have very precise roles and very structured 'hierarchies'. Information and instructions will be passed down the organisation in a formal way, the most senior manager to his or her subordinate(s), who in turn will pass this to their subordinates. This is called a 'chain of command'.	
Other organisations may have one person (or a small group of people) at the centre of the organisation passing out information and instructions to everyone else. This is much less formal and decisions are made more quickly.	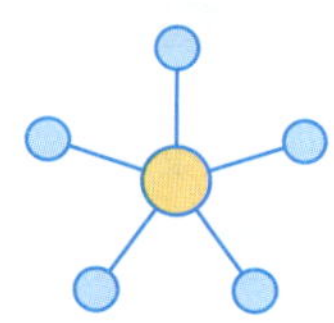
Sometimes the favoured culture of an organisation is a 'team culture', where tasks are taken on by groups of people working together for a particular task.	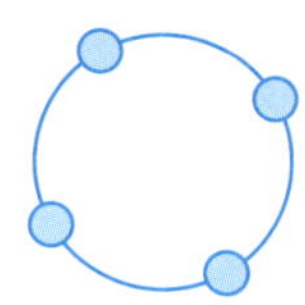
Some organisations have a culture of equality. They place the same value on each employee regardless of their position.	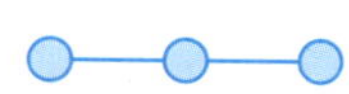

ACTIVITIES

TASK 1

Like many other organisations, schools have a set of values and everyone in the school – students and staff – will be expected to act in a way that is appropriate to the values. A typical value is: *We are respectful towards each other*.
With a partner, make a list of values at the centre of your school's culture.

TASK 2

You are a manager of a supermarket. It has been brought to your attention that some members of staff have not been following the values that you consider to be important to the culture of the supermarket. For example, a customer reported having been kept waiting at the kiosk while two staff members chatted.

With a partner, prepare a statement from management reminding staff of the values at the heart of your organisation.

TASK 3

Some organisations see a policy of wearing a uniform as being important to their culture.

- Make a list of organisations you know of which have a uniform policy.
- Write down your thoughts on why they have this uniform policy.

MAKE THE LINK

- Your school has a culture. Some schools will have quite an informal attitude to uniform, while others have a strict uniform policy. However, one thing all schools have in common is expectations inside and outside the school. There are likely to be rules in every classroom so that we act respectfully towards each other and approach work appropriately.

DID YOU KNOW?

Nowadays many people support the Fairtrade movement. However, you may not know that it is possible to become a fair trade school and join the growing number of schools who adopt the fair trade message in their culture. Visit http://www.scottishfairtradeforum.org.uk/schools to find out more.

OUR EVERYDAY LIVES

We are all familiar with the Body Shop brand in our high streets and shopping centres. What you may not realise is that values have always been important to the Body Shop, from their respect for individuals, to their concern for the future of the planet. Go online and look at the website for the Body Shop. Are you convinced by their values or do you simply believe it is clever marketing?

TASK 4

Some organisations do not allow individuals within the organisations to wear religious symbols, such as a cross. Discuss with a partner possible reasons for including this rule in their culture.

INTERDISCIPLINARY PROJECT

THE CULTURE OF AN ORGANISATION

If managers do not think the culture at the heart of their organisation is important, it is unlikely that the organisation will be successful. If, for example, a culture of mistrust is allowed to dominate in an organisation, the staff will be less inclined to work for the good of the organisation.

EXAMPLE

Gail's Hair Design is a hair salon in the Scottish Borders. The salon benefits from being the only business of its kind within a twenty-mile radius, meaning that it is heavily booked most of the time. It would seem that this is a business with a positive future – but on further investigation, all is not well.

Gail, the owner of the salon, is seldom present, preferring to spend time in her other salons in Edinburgh and Glasgow. A manager, Annie Wilkinson, runs the salon. Miss Wilkinson, as she is known, has a 'need to know' policy, meaning she only lets the stylists know about what directly affects them. The result is a culture of mistrust and resentment.

Gary, an experienced stylist who has worked in the salon for nine years, confronted the manager accusing her of favouritism. According to Gary, Annie's niece, Tia, who qualified as a stylist last year, gets the best shifts and the pick of her day off. Gary is informed of his day off, often with only twenty-four hours' notice. He has never had a choice of day since Annie became manager. Gary has tried to contact Gail to discuss the problems at the salon with her but she is never available. Gary doesn't know if the other stylists share his feelings as Annie disapproves of the stylists engaging in discussion. Gary is thinking of leaving and opening a new salon in direct competition. It is likely that his regular clients would go with him.

In a group of three, produce a report containing a plan to change the culture of this organisation. Consider the following three areas:

- existing problems
- consequences of allowing the present situation to continue
- your recommendations for change in the organisation.

To divide the workload, once you have agreed on its content, each group member should type or write one section of the report.

MAKE THE LINK

- In many, if not all, subjects we are encouraged to work in teams.

ACTIVITIES

TASK 1

Some organisations see the benefit of holding an annual staff 'away day'. This is usually a trip, perhaps to the coast, and staff from all parts of the organisation are invited to take part. It is an opportunity to spend time with colleagues in a non-work environment. However, during a recession some organisations may feel they cannot justify the cost of such an event.

Your workmates have nominated you to write to the management of your organisation in response to an announcement that the annual day trip is to be cancelled because of difficult economic circumstances. Include all the reasons you can think of why the trip should go ahead. Don't just think about the benefits to the employees – include reasons why you believe it would harm the organisation as a whole if the trip were cancelled.

TASK 2

An expression that is often used is 'reward culture'. This means that an employee's loyalty and willingness to work hard is rewarded, possibly by being promoted. The reward may be financial, for example a pay rise or a bonus. The organisation may even reward employees with shares, meaning they become part owners of the organisation.

With a partner, discuss why an organisation may well benefit from rewarding employees with shares.

TASK 3

Link-IT plc was floated on the stock market last year. Amanda Crawford was rewarded with 1000 £1 shares. After a year her shares have gone up in value by 14%. Amanda also received a share dividend, which is 5% of the present share value.

1. Calculate the present value of Amanda's shares.
2. Calculate the amount of the dividend paid to Amanda.

MY LEARNING CHECKLIST

Put a tick in the column to show how you think you got on with each statement.
Green means you got on really well with your learning in this area.
Amber means you did well with your learning.
Red means you need to do a bit of work on your learning.

	Good to go!	Getting there	Help needed
1. ***I understand that an organisation is wise to work towards a positive organisational culture.***	○	○	○
2. ***I understand the benefits to be gained from a positive culture.***	○	○	○
3. ***I understand that benefits to a local community can also benefit an organisation.***	○	○	○
4. ***I understand that rewarding employees can make them feel valued.***	○	○	○
5. ***I understand how to calculate a percentage.***	○	○	○

ORGANISATIONS ACTING RESPONSIBLY

Organisations work towards being as effective as possible. In the case of the private sector, an important aim is to make as high a profit as possible. However, often the way to a high profit can involve disadvantaging stakeholders, in particular employees. If, for example, a large organisation kept its costs down by paying its employees at a very low rate, it would be accused of earning high profits at the expense of its workers.

In the UK, the **Minimum Wage Act** protects workers from low pay. An organisation may move its operations overseas to avoid this law, but if a newspaper report brings this to the attention of the organisation's customers or stakeholders, its popularity could be affected. Successful organisations will, therefore, take steps to avoid acting in a way considered irresponsible or unfair.

TOP TIP

A programme called Zero Waste Scotland provides individuals and organisations with support and advice to help with the reduction of waste. The Scottish Government, in common with other governments worldwide, realise that continuing to use our scarce resources inefficiently will lead to big problems for future generations.

Apart from possible bad publicity associated with acting irresponsibly, staff may develop resentment for an employer acting in this way and may look for employment elsewhere.

ACTIVITIES

TASK 1

A company called Simply Ecosse makes and distributes novelty gifts to tourist gift shops around Scotland. However, it has come to your attention that the gifts are no longer made in Scotland. The company has the gifts made in South East Asia to take advantage of the lower wage rate of workers. The company defends itself by stating that it is bringing jobs to an area in great need. It also makes the point that the workers produce the items to a high standard. Nevertheless, you have decided to write an article for a newspaper to inform the public of the actions of this company. You should write in a way that will grab the attention of readers. However, you should be careful to give a balanced report to the reader. Include a suitable headline.

TASK 2

Most organisations nowadays do what they can to reduce waste. This makes good economic sense for organisations but they may also be aware that wasting the world's scarce resources is considered to be irresponsible.

With a partner, discuss ways of reducing waste in your school, from the school office to the cafeteria. The slogan 'reduce, reuse, recycle' will help you to think of ways of wasting less.

TASK 3

Another way an organisation can be responsible is by 'giving back' to the area in which it operates. For example, an organisation may recognise that it has benefited from being in a certain area, perhaps because its local residents have tolerated the effects of a large organisation being on their doorstep over a number of years.

Discuss with a partner:

1. How a community might be disadvantaged by a large organisation operating in the local area.
2. Ways in which an organisation could give back to a community.

This would be a good topic for a class discussion.

MAKE THE LINK

- In **Geography**, we learn about multinational organisations.
- In **English**, we learn how to write in an interesting and engaging way.

DID YOU KNOW?

British Petroleum (BP) was heavily criticised in 2010 in the wake of the oil spill in the Gulf of Mexico, which had a serious environmental impact. Although this has often been called irresponsible, BP is also known for providing teaching resources for use in schools and colleges in the UK. This could be described as a responsible action.

OUR EVERYDAY LIVES

The Royal Bank of Scotland is a familiar brand to us all. We see RBS in high streets all over Scotland and the rest of the UK. It is a name which has been trusted for many years. However, in 2008 the UK government of the day had to invest in RBS, which (along with other banks) had made business decisions which led to the bank losing a great deal of money. This has been called irresponsible and the British economy will feel the impact of it for years to come.

INTERDISCIPLINARY PROJECT

ORGANISATIONS ACTING RESPONSIBLY

Most organisations nowadays are familiar with the term 'social responsibility' and many of them take steps to be socially responsible. Organisations and individuals are encouraged to be 'waste aware' but that is just one part of the message. We could say that social responsibility is being mindful of the future of our planet, including all of its inhabitants.

John Wells of the Moonset Function Suite has asked a firm of consultants, who are experts on social responsibility, for advice. The consultants have arranged to visit the premises.

This project involves you writing, producing and performing a five-minute play, acting out the meeting between John and the two consultants. In a group of three:

- Decide on the advice to be given. As your play will be five minutes long, limit your advice to **two** or at the most **three** areas. Remember the kind of business the Moonset Function Suite is and deal with issues directly related to the business.
- Write a script with lines for all three actors.
- Take care to structure your play: for example, start with introductions and an explanation of why social responsibility is so important in business. Ensure that the play has a well-crafted ending.
- Make sure you run to time.
- You must take time to rehearse and learn your lines. This may be done outside class, perhaps after school or at lunchtime.
- Perform your play.

Perhaps your plays could be performed at school assemblies.

MAKE THE LINK

- In classes, but also in the wider school and beyond, we are encouraged to be 'socially aware': for example, we are discouraged from dropping litter and we are encouraged to reduce, reuse and recycle paper, packaging and other materials.

ACTIVITIES

TASK 1

For many years, producers of various products have paid a lot of attention to the way their products are packaged. In a group of three, choose three popular products. For each of your choices, think about ways the packaging could be made to be more socially responsible.

- Product 1 should have less bulky (reduced) packaging.
- Product 2 should have packaging which could be reused.
- Product 3 should have packaging which could be recycled.

This could be made into a presentation.

TASK 2

We are concerned nowadays about the 'carbon footprint' of products. Often, products transported for miles could be produced much closer to their market.

- Make a list of products produced locally in your area.
- Suggest how the local market could be encouraged to buy more of this product.

TASK 3

Happy Babies, a company that makes a range of environmentally friendly bath products for infants, aims to reduce its packaging by 12%. It estimates that this will reduce packaging costs by one fifth (0·2). Expressed as a percentage this is 20%.

Given that the cost of the container for its bubble bath is at present 35 pence, calculate the cost of the container once the policy of package reduction has been introduced.

MY LEARNING CHECKLIST

Put a tick in the column to show how you think you got on with each statement.
Green means you got on really well with your learning in this area.
Amber means you did well with your learning.
Red means you need to do a bit of work on your learning.

	Good to go!	Getting there	Help needed
1. *I understand that organisations see being socially responsible as a way of contributing to their success.*	○	○	○
2. *I understand that buying locally-sourced products is increasing in popularity.*	○	○	○
3. *I understand that reducing the amount of packaging used can also reduce a company's costs.*	○	○	○
4. *I understand that reduced packaging is popular with consumers.*	○	○	○
5. *I know how to express a fraction as a percentage.*	○	○	○

PEOPLE IN ORGANISATIONS 1

The vast majority of the population will, at some point in their lives, be part of the workforce. They may work for an employer or be self-employed but they will all contribute to the production of goods or services, which will be useful or give enjoyment to others.

TOP TIP

Having fewer layers in an organisation can be good for communication. Information can be passed up and down the organisation without delay. In some organisations it is particularly important that there are no delays in communication to help speed up the decision-making process.

There are different reasons why people work. Some examples are:

- to make a living
- to be sociable with workmates
- to get job satisfaction
- to give life structure and meaning
- to gain new skills.

Although many people might call workmates, 'friends', others do not have social relationships with people they work with. However, if they are able to work well together and have respect for one other, it doesn't matter that they don't have a relationship that goes beyond the workplace.

It is important that relationships between workmates are clearly understood. This is useful for stakeholders: for example, an interviewee for a job may find it helpful to know the identity of their immediate boss (line manager) in case they get the job.

ACTIVITIES

TASK 1

INVITE ME!

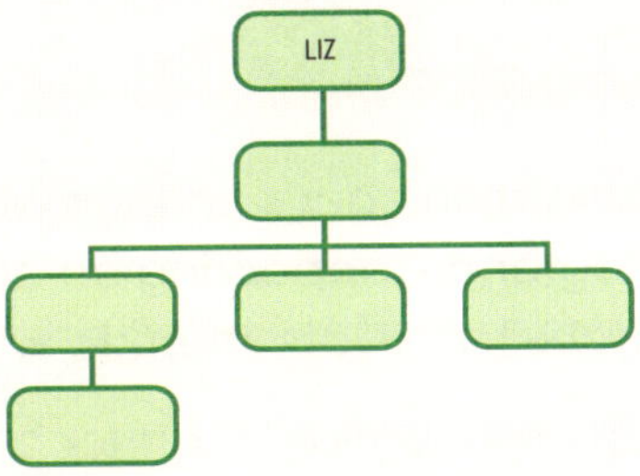

The image shows a diagram called an **organisation chart.** Each rectangle should have an employee's name in it and possibly the employee's job title and photograph.

The company called Invite Me! has a managing director called Liz Newman who is most senior in the organisation (as shown). The office manager, Alan Banks, is directly answerable to Liz Newman. Three officers are directly answerable to Alan. They are Jordan Kelly (finance officer), Erin Lang (sales officer) and Jay Smart (purchasing officer). Jordan Kelly has a finance assistant, Sarah Gray, immediately answerable to him.

Copy the organisation chart and insert all the correct information in the appropriate rectangles. This is a task that could be done on the computer.

TASK 2

1. Employees on the same level have a **lateral** relationship. Write down the names of the employees in Invite Me! who have a lateral relationship.
2. A **line** relationship can be followed up or down the organisation. Write down (a) the name of Sarah's line manager; (b) the name of Jay's line manager; and (c) the name of Alan's line manager.

TASK 3

'Span of control' refers to the number of people a manager is in direct control of. Although Liz is the most senior in the organisation, she has only one person in her span of control: Alan.

1. Who is in Jordan's span of control?
2. Who is in Alan's span of control?

TASK 4

You are the manager in control of an organisation producing computer games. You want to fill the jobs of:

- production manager
- sales manager
- finance manager.

Each of your three department managers will have one assistant.

- Think of a good name for the company, which should appear at the top of a page above the words **organisation chart**.
- Choose students in your class for each job. Think about who would be suitable.
- Draw an organisation chart for everyone working in your organisation, including each employee's name and job title.

MAKE THE LINK

- In various subjects, we use diagrams to show relationships.
- In **Social Education**, we learn about the world of work.

DID YOU KNOW?

In February 2011, the Scottish Government introduced the **Protecting Vulnerable Groups Scheme**. The scheme helps to ensure that those having regular contact with children and protected adults through paid and unpaid work do not have a known history of harmful behaviour. The scheme makes it easier for employers to decide on individuals who need to be checked. The scheme speeds up the process of disclosure without making it less thorough.

OUR EVERYDAY LIVES

In years to come, it is very likely that you will be interviewed for a job. It would be wise to have a look at the organisation chart of the company to get an idea about who works there and what they do. This is an important piece of an organisation's internal information, which may appear on the organisation's website or on a wall in their reception area.

INTERDISCIPLINARY PROJECT

PEOPLE IN ORGANISATIONS 1

Many organisations, even small ones, display organisation charts on their walls or websites. A new employee seeing their name – and perhaps photograph – appearing on an organisation chart is likely to feel part of that organisation and this may well motivate them to work hard.

This project involves you and a partner creating an organisation chart for a department in your school, or perhaps the senior management team or the office staff. Your teacher will suggest a department for you so that every pair has a different one.

- To get full details of the employees in the department, interview the head of the department. Explain to the head of department what you would like to do. Ask if they would allow you to create the chart and, if so, if they would supply you with the details you require to make the chart.
- Once you have permission to make the chart, plan it on scrap paper or on the computer.
- Each employee in the department should be shown on the chart. **Line** and **lateral** relationships should be clear. Include names and job titles. It may also be possible to add photographs if you have access to a digital camera and permission to take photographs for this purpose.
- You can decide between you how you will present your chart. An A3 piece of coloured card would work well as a base. If you have an A3 laminator in school, laminate the chart to protect it when it is complete. You could use large stencils for the name of the department and smaller ones for the names and job titles of the staff.

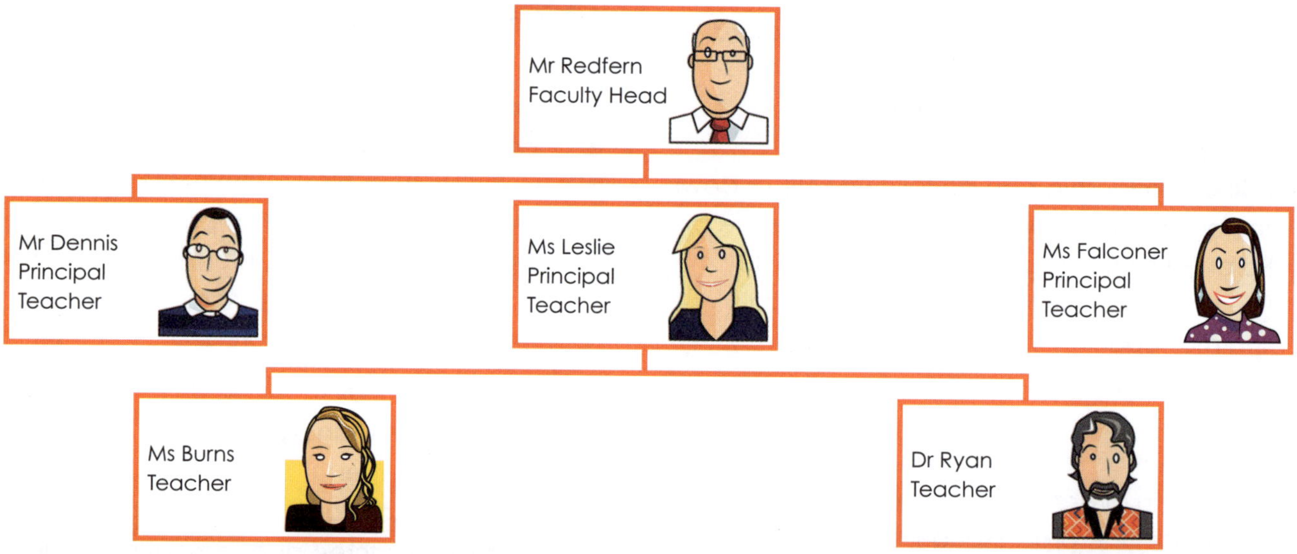

MAKE THE LINK

- We learn about how workers are protected in **Modern Studies**.
- We learn about the process of applying for jobs in **Social Education**.

ACTIVITIES

TASK 1

The Scottish Government makes many decisions affecting the citizens of Scotland. The First Minister is at the head of government. In the span of control of the First Minister are the Finance Secretary, the Justice Secretary, the Health Secretary and the Education Secretary. Find out the names of all five of these politicians and create an organisation chart showing how they relate to each other. You could possibly find photographs online to include in your chart. You might even find out about members of the government who have a line relationship to each of the secretaries and add these names to your chart.

TASK 2

Your organisation is looking for a finance officer who will line directly to the finance manager. Make a list of places where this job could be advertised.

TASK 3

Five candidates will be interviewed for the job of finance officer. Discuss with a partner four questions which will be put to each of the candidates. Remember, it is important to find out as much as you can about the suitability of the candidate for the job.

TASK 4

Before a candidate is appointed, it is important that certain documents are shown to the organisation or brought to the interview to confirm that the candidate is **suitable** and **eligible** for the job: for example, the candidate's passport to confirm their identity. Make a list of other documents that must be shown before a candidate is taken on.

MY LEARNING CHECKLIST

Put a tick in the column to show how you think you got on with each statement.
Green means you got on really well with your learning in this area.
Amber means you did well with your learning.
Red means you need to do a bit of work on your learning.

	Good to go!	Getting there	Help needed
1. *I know why organisations display organisation charts.*	○	○	○
2. *I understand the difference between a line and a lateral relationship.*	○	○	○
3. *I understand that a selection procedure, often an interview, will be carried out before a candidate is appointed to a job.*	○	○	○
4. *I understand the reasons why people work.*	○	○	○
5. *I understand that a manager's span of control relates to the subordinates in his or her direct control.*	○	○	○

PEOPLE IN ORGANISATIONS 2

In organisations, it is important that various stakeholders communicate well with one other. This could be two employees communicating over lunch or it could be a meeting of shareholders unhappy about the way an organisation is being run by its board of directors. In both of these cases, good communication will benefit the organisation. Similarly, good communication between an employee and their line manager is crucial.

TOP TIP
It is important to consider the receiver of information you are passing on. Friends of your own age may well understand expressions you use frequently but older people will be unfamiliar with such language. It is also important to remember an appropriate level of formality. Using 'text speak' when applying for a job definitely would not go down well!

EXAMPLE

British Airways (BA) is a British company with a high global profile. However, in recent times BA has experienced considerable problems, one of which is the disagreement between staff and management over pay and conditions of work. Many of the cabin crew of BA are represented by a union called Unite. A trade union looks after the interests of its members, and union officials hold talks with management on behalf of union members to try to reach a fair settlement for the employees. This communication is vital for the smooth running of BA. Equally, however, much less formal communication is important in organisations.

Some other examples of communication in an organisation are:

- a line manager holding a review meeting (appraisal) with an employee about the employee's progress and future in the organisation
- a staff meeting keeping staff briefed about upcoming changes
- internal online information informing staff of current job opportunities.

ACTIVITIES

TASK 1

A job appraisal review is carried out regularly to ensure an employee's performance is the best it can be. Think about your year in school up to now. Write down what you think you have done well and what you believe you must improve on.

TASK 2

The passage about BA refers to Unite, a union representing airline workers. Carry out some research to find out the names of at least two other unions. Write down the name of the union and the kind of workers they represent.

TASK 3

Look at the following extracts from conversations between stakeholders in Invite Me! Discuss with a partner who the conversation might be between:

1. 'Welcome to Invite Me! Please have a seat. Firstly, could you tell me what talents you could bring to this company?'
2. 'I hear the office might be closing early on Christmas Eve. Do you think that's true?'
3. 'I have an emergency dental appointment today at 3 o'clock. Could I please have permission to leave work early?'

TASK 4

Sometimes factors can get in the way of good communication. We call these 'communication barriers'. One example might be that a manager speaks to an employee using very technical language that the employee does not understand.

Think of a time when you found it difficult to receive information. Write down some examples of barriers to good communication.

MAKE THE LINK

- In **Modern Studies**, we learn about the work of unions.
- In **English**, we learn how to write plays.

DID YOU KNOW?

Industrial action only takes place if the sides (union and management) in a negotiation cannot reach agreement. For example, the workers may have a **work to rule**, which is when they do their contracted job – and absolutely nothing else. In the most extreme circumstances, they may withdraw their labour completely, i.e. **go on strike**.

OUR EVERYDAY LIVES

In 2010, government statistics showed that in the UK there were 7 million union members, with two out of three being in the public sector. Cuts being made by the coalition government will hit jobs in the public sector. However, the public sector uses many services in the private sector, so the private sector is likely to suffer too. Added to this, more unemployed people may mean that businesses sell less. Nevertheless, the coalition government stands by its decision to make cuts. The UK has borrowed a great deal of money in recent years and the government believes cutting public services is a way of reducing the UK's debt.

INTERDISCIPLINARY PROJECT

PEOPLE IN ORGANISATIONS 2

When the representatives (reps) of a trade union and the management of an organisation cannot agree on pay and conditions of employees, we might say they have reached 'stalemate'. This expression from the game of chess means that neither player can continue to play. They are effectively blocked.

In this project, you have to get into groups of four. Two of you will be trade union officials and the other two will be members of the management team of the company who will meet to negotiate a pay rise. The situation is that the management is offering a 2% pay rise to all workers. The union reps believe this is not reasonable because the company's profits were high last year and are forecast to be even higher this year. However, the management is worried about the economic recession and see it as unwise to increase pay by a larger amount at such an uncertain time.

TOP TIP

A trade union does of course have its members' interests at heart and consequently may fight for a good wage rise for members. However, in these difficult economic times, it should be remembered that a high pay claim may cause an organisation's costs to rise to the extent that it cannot stay competitive and may ultimately fail.

The two union officials should discuss the points they want to make in their meeting with management. Take a note of the points. Divide the points to be made between both reps. The managers should do likewise, ensuring that each manager has strong arguments to put to the union officials about why they must keep control of the annual pay rise.

However, both sides must also decide how far they are prepared to go to come to an agreement with the other side.

Once you have reached an agreement, write down what you have agreed. All four group members should sign the agreement.

MAKE THE LINK

- In **Modern Studies**, we learn about the work of unions.
- In **English**, we learn how to write plays.

ACTIVITIES

TASK 1

Iain Stark used to be paid a flat wage of £21 000 in his job as a financial adviser for a bank. This year his basic pay was cut from £21 000 to £19 000 plus commission. Iain earns 1.5% in commission for every product he sells. In the year since the new pay structure was brought in, Iain has sold £30 000 of products. Showing your working, decide whether Iain is better or worse off under the new scheme.

TASK 2

Iain worked overtime last year. He worked an extra 107 hours at a rate of £11.60 per hour. No commission was paid for these hours. Calculate the extra pay earned by Iain from working the extra hours.

TASK 3

Banks, like other organisations, receive complaints and will have a department dealing with them and putting them right. If the bank wants to retain their customers, and avoid bad publicity, it is important that customer complaints are dealt with effectively.

Discuss with a partner typical complaints a bank might receive and what they could do to put the complaints right.

MY LEARNING CHECKLIST

Put a tick in the column to show how you think you got on with each statement.
Green means you got on really well with your learning in this area.
Amber means you did well with your learning.
Red means you need to do a bit of work on your learning.

	Good to go!	Getting there	Help needed
1. *I understand the difference between being paid a wage and being paid commission.*	○	○	○
2. *I understand the term 'overtime'.*	○	○	○
3. *I understand the importance of organisations attending to complaints.*	○	○	○
4. *I understand the importance of communication in organisations.*	○	○	○
5. *I understand the importance of a job appraisal review (JAR).*	○	○	○

PEOPLE IN ORGANISATIONS 3

How can organisations get the right person for the right job? Often problems can arise, not because the worker is short on skills or ability, but because they are simply wrong for the job they are employed to do. This can be likened to trying to put a square peg into a round hole.

Part of the job of an organisation's **human resources department** is to ensure that the person they select for a job is the right fit.

They do this by:

- advertising the job in an upbeat way, without exaggerating the description of the job
- paying close attention to the application submitted by each applicant
- carrying out a thorough selection process, for example interviews
- checking documents properly, for example references from former employers, qualifications and, in some cases, police checks to make sure the candidate would be suitable to work with vulnerable groups.

TOP TIP

Jobs in sales advertised in the media sometimes state 'OTE £50 000 per year'. This sounds very attractive but beware. OTE stands for **opportunity to earn**. This tells you that the job is based on commission, meaning that the employee's earnings are linked to their level of sales. It may be possible to earn £50 000 per year, but it is probably unlikely that the employee will reach this level of pay.

Distribution Operative SPD

SPD Industries are seeking a bright and motivated individual to join the team. This post offers challenge and reward. The successful candidate will be heavily involved in the distribution of key items of documentation within the organisation and also to stakeholders outside the organisation.

You may be surprised to know that the above post is actually for a messenger. While there is undoubtedly value in a job like this, the wording of the advert would give the impression that there is more to it than there actually is. This will attract the wrong applicants and is a waste of time for everyone.

ACTIVITIES

TASK 1

Rewrite the job advertisement so that it attracts the right applicants.

TASK 2

- It is common practice for organisations to issue application forms for posts so that applicants can provide them with all the necessary information needed to decide whether they should be taken forward to the next stage, for example an interview.
- A job description will also be issued setting out in detail all the tasks which must be undertaken by the successful candidate.
- A person specification may also be included, which will give conditions that the successful candidate **must** meet (essentials) and conditions the employer **would like** them to meet (desirables).
- Nowadays, the above process often happens online.

Create an application form for the applicants of the messenger job to complete, taking care to include relevant questions that will help you to decide whether the applicant should be interviewed.

TASK 3

Make a list of **essentials** and a list of **desirables** to be included in the **person specification** for the messenger job.

TASK 4

Which of the following tasks do you think would be included in a job description for the job of messenger?

1. Deliver items to different departments in the organisation.
2. Answer telephone calls and greet customers to the building.
3. Organise items into a suitable order ready for delivery.
4. Deliver items to local organisations.
5. Ensure that delivered items are signed for.
6. Ensure that the reception area of the organisation is kept in good order.

MAKE THE LINK

- In **Social Education**, we learn about the process of applying for jobs.
- In **English**, we learn how to write using appropriate language.

DID YOU KNOW?

Although employees are entitled to a contract, which sets out the terms of their employment, such as pay and hours of work, that contract will not necessarily be permanent. More and more in the current uncertain economic times, employers are giving employees temporary contracts. As a class, discuss reasons why the contract given may be temporary.

OUR EVERYDAY LIVES

After several high-profile cases of employees abusing children and other vulnerable groups, it was recognised by government that potential employees likely to come into contact with such groups, should go through a process to check their suitability for the job. In Scotland, this process is called Disclosure Scotland. For example, anyone applying to do any job in a school cannot take up the job until they had been cleared through this process.

In February 2011, the Scottish Government introduced the **Protecting Vulnerable Groups Scheme** with regard to people who work with vulnerable people. Any person who is a member of this scheme will not have to go through the disclosure procedure every time they get a new job involving working with vulnerable groups. It will be enough for a prospective employer to check to see if the person is a member of the scheme. As a class, you could discuss groups which might be considered to be vulnerable.

INTERDISCIPLINARY PROJECT

PEOPLE IN ORGANISATIONS 3

When candidates have been selected to be interviewed, the questions that they will be asked must be decided upon. Each candidate must be asked exactly the same questions and will be scored based on their responses. The candidate with the highest score, when all questions have been asked and answered, is called the 'preferred candidate' and will be offered the job, subject to various checks.

The purpose of this project is to choose a student who is suitable to be a class rep and represent the class on the School Council.

Get into teams of six. There will be four interviewers, two pairs of two. The remaining two will be interviewed for the position of class rep. One pair of interviewers will interview candidate 1 and the other pair will interview candidate 2. At the end of these interviews, each candidate will then be interviewed by the other pair of interviewers.

Before the interviews take place, the interviewers should decide on the questions to be asked. You can ask either four or five questions. You cannot ask the candidate personal questions, such as about their home life, but you can ask them questions about what makes them a good candidate for the position.

While the interviewers are agreeing on the questions to be asked, the candidates should use the time to jot down some notes about why they would make a good class rep. For example, you may want to include that you have good language skills and are able to make good points.

After about ten minutes, the interviews should begin. The interviewers should take note of the candidates' responses and a mark of between 1 and 5 should be given for each response. The interview should last between five and ten minutes.

After both candidates have been interviewed by both sets of interviewers, the scores from each interview should be added together to find the successful candidate – the one with the highest overall score.

Each pair of interviewers should announce to the rest of the class:

- the names of the two candidates interviewed
- who the preferred candidate is and why this candidate stood out.

Note: If your class does not divide evenly by six, some interviewing teams can have three interviewers.

MAKE THE LINK

- We learn about the world of work in **Social Education**.
- We learn about changes in the workforce over years in **History** and **Modern Studies**.

ACTIVITIES

TASK 1

Apart from interviews, there are other ways of selecting candidates. In some cases, it may be appropriate for candidates to sit a test. For example, a trainee assistant for a finance department may have to sit a numeracy test to assess their suitability.

Create a test with between five and ten number-based questions. At least two of your questions should be scenarios, for example: *A customer buys fifty packets of A4 paper at £2.50 per packet, but returns eighteen packets. How much does the customer now owe the firm?*

Make the difficulty of your questions appropriate.

After about ten minutes, swap tests with a partner. After your partner has completed the test, take the test back and check their answers. Are they good enough to get the job?

TASK 2

1. Make a list of other tests that could be taken and state the kind of job the test would suit.
2. Can you think of any other ways of selecting the right candidates, other than interviews or tests?

TASK 3

It is important to get references from previous employers before a new employee is taken on. Discuss with a partner reasons why checking references is so important.

TASK 4

The new employee is entitled to a contract of employment. Make a list of what would be included in a contract.

MY LEARNING CHECKLIST

Put a tick in the column to show how you think you got on with each statement.
Green means you got on really well with your learning in this area.
Amber means you did well with your learning.
Red means you need to do a bit of work on your learning.

	Good to go!	Getting there	Help needed
1. ***I understand the importance of finding the right candidate to employ in an organisation.***	◯	◯	◯
2. ***I understand the importance of job descriptions and person specifications.***	◯	◯	◯
3. ***I understand the importance of carrying out an interview properly.***	◯	◯	◯
4. ***I know why candidates may be tested for certain skills.***	◯	◯	◯
5. ***I understand why it is important to check references (and other documents) before taking on a new employee.***	◯	◯	◯

MARKETING 1 – RESEARCHING AND SEGMENTING THE MARKET

The purpose of market research is to find out information that will tell an organisation what it is doing wrong – and right. This will help the organisation to improve in the future. Businesses carry out research to find out what customers want.

EXAMPLE

Invite Me! is considering extending its product range. Mindful of Scotland's diverse cultural mix, the idea is to introduce cards for occasions such as the celebration of a Bar Mitzvah. The question is, will there be enough interest in the cards to justify the expensive artwork and other costs involved? For this reason, research will be carried out. Existing customers will be asked to complete an online questionnaire. The questions must be clear to avoid confusion and be worded in a way that gives useful answers.

TOP TIP

Be careful when wording questions for a survey. You may be tempted to ask a question that only requires a yes or no answer, but this may limit responses. The respondent may well have something else to say that would have been useful for your research.

ACTIVITIES

TASK 1

With a partner, do some research online to find out about other celebrations which *Invite Me!* may consider including in their range. The first one has been done for you:

Celebration	Description
Bar Mitzvah	At age 13, a Jewish boy will go through a ceremony that recognises that he has become an adult who is responsible for his own actions.

ACTIVITIES

TASK 2

Along with one or two others, come up with six questions appropriate for the survey. Swap your finished questions with another team. Consider the other team's questions. Are they right for the survey? If not, discuss with your teammates any weaknesses in the question(s) and suggest appropriate rewording.

TASK 3

If marketing is to be carried out effectively, it is essential that groups of consumers are targeted. For example stairlifts are advertised on television during shows that are popular with older people because stairlift producers know that this market group (or **segment**) is most likely to buy the product. This is called **market segmentation**.

Through research, Invite Me! has found that school proms are becoming popular. This is an American tradition of high school students holding a grand party to mark the end of their school life. Students invite guests, such as teachers or Parent Council members. Invite Me! is going to develop online invitations for school proms.

1. Bearing in mind who will be organising a school prom, decide with a partner an appropriate market segment to target with this new product.
2. Design a one-page advert for the new product. Use language and images that are appropriate for the market segment being targeted.

TASK 4

Look at the following ways of segmenting a market. Break the markets down into segments. The first one has been done for you:

Segmented By	Groups
Level of earnings	Under £10 000 per year; £10 000–£30 000 per year; Over £30 000 per year
Age	
Gender	
Ethnic group	

MAKE THE LINK

- We learn about designing products in **CDT** and **Art & Design**.
- We learn about different religions in **RME**.
- We learn about respecting other religions and ethnic groups in **Social Education**.
- In **English**, we learn about using different language to relate to different readers.

DID YOU KNOW?

People are now living to a much older age. Many older people use the internet to buy products. Businesses classify this market segment as 'silver surfers' – and they know these people are worth targeting. Often people in this market segment are financially able to spend on products. They also have more time to shop. Many businesses exist specifically for older people. An example is *Saga Holidays*. It sells holidays designed particularly for the older holidaymaker. This company has also moved into other products designed for the older consumer. If you have time you could research this company to find out about their other products.

OUR EVERYDAY LIVES

The charity, *Oxfam*, carried out research online which indicated that many people would send fewer Christmas cards in 2010 than they did in 2005. Reasons given were concern for the environment and saving money. The research also showed that people over the age of 55 are much more likely to send Christmas cards than young people. Christmas card selling has been a major source of fundraising for charities for many years so this is bad news for *Oxfam*. The charity may have to think of other ways of raising funds.

INTERDISCIPLINARY PROJECT

MARKETING 1 – RESEARCHING AND SEGMENTING THE MARKET

Marketers use a technique called 'consumer profiling'. This allows them to describe their target customer. Knowing the type of person they want to sell the product to enables companies to design their product exactly for that target customer.

In this project, you will make a wall display showing various people (famous or not famous) surrounded by facts that define and describe them. For example, if you were to choose tennis player Andrew Murray, you would find a picture of him online or in a newspaper or magazine. His picture could be surrounded with the facts shown below.

The large heading at the top of your display should read: Consumer profiles. Include a range of target consumers, all surrounded with different facts.

MAKE THE LINK

- We learn about the free movement of labour around the EU in **Modern Studies** and **Geography**.
- We learn about the use of language in **English**.

ACTIVITIES

TASK 1

Consumer profiling is very useful for making the best use of advertising. Discuss with a partner how consumer profiling could make advertising more effective. Consider, for example, where and when adverts appear.

TASK 2

The following advert has been written to appeal to a woman in her sixties. The advert is for fresh orange juice. Reword the advert so that it appeals to a teenage boy.

Sunblush is a fresh and delicious drink. It is packed with vitamins and minerals to help you get all the nutrition you need to stay well, fit and young at heart. Try it today!

TASK 3

Television advertising is very effective. Look at the list of target customers shown below and suggest a TV show that they are likely to watch.

1. Man, aged thirty-five, mid-range earner, sports fan.
2. Boy, aged twelve, likes computer games.
3. Girl, aged eighteen, student, likes chart music.
4. Woman, aged fifty, nurse, goes to the gym.

TASK 4

In recent years, migrant workers from Poland and other countries have settled in Scotland. Supermarkets have responded by targeting this market. It is quite usual to see a display of foods enjoyed by this target market to encourage them to shop in that supermarket. We describe a group like this as an 'ethnic minority'.

Can you think of other ethnic minorities who have settled in Scotland? Think about products which would be purchased by the ethnic minority.

This would be a good activity for a class discussion.

MY LEARNING CHECKLIST

Put a tick in the column to show how you think you got on with each statement.
Green means you got on really well with your learning in this area.
Amber means you did well with your learning.
Red means you need to do a bit of work on your learning.

		Good to go!	Getting there	Help needed
1.	*I know that there is a range of segments in a market.*	○	○	○
2.	*I understand that research is useful to organisations in different sectors.*	○	○	○
3.	*I understand the purpose of consumer profiling.*	○	○	○
4.	*I understand that feedback from research can lead to improvements being made in services.*	○	○	○
5.	*I understand that television advertising is very effective.*	○	○	○

MARKETING 2 – THE MARKETING MIX

To carry out marketing successfully, the process is divided into 4 parts. This is known as **the marketing mix** or **the 4 P's**.

Price considers the selling price of a product. If the price is wrong, one or more of the following problems will arise:

- The product won't be attractive to the right market segment.
- The product won't be able to compete with other similar products.
- The price won't be enough to cover costs and make a profit.

Product considers the good or service being sold. If the content or appearance of a product is wrong, one or more of the following problems will arise:

- The product won't be attractive to the right market segment.
- The product won't be able to compete with other similar products.
- The product's popularity will be short-lived.

Place considers where a product will be sold. If a product is not sold in (or from) an appropriate place, one or more of the following problems will arise:

- The product won't be noticed by the right market segment.
- The selling costs will be too high to make a reasonable profit.
- The product's image may be damaged.

Promotion considers how the public will be made aware of a product, for example by advertising or sponsorship. If the promotion of a product is not managed properly, one or more of the following problems will arise:

- The product won't attract the attention of consumers.
- Consumers will get a confused message about the product.
- The spending on advertising/sponsorship will not be good value for money.

EXAMPLE

When Graeme Robb was made redundant from his job as an IT specialist for a major bank, he decided that he wanted to develop his hobby and go into business offering a gardening service. He used the small amount of redundancy pay he received to buy a petrol lawn mower and some new gardening tools. Graeme printed some leaflets, which he delivered around homes in his local area giving details of his service.

Within a few days Graeme had received several enquiries. He quoted prices for all of the enquiring customers based on the length of time he estimated it would take to carry out the job. He was dismayed to find, however, that no quote was accepted. This, it transpired, was because a competing gardening service offered a more attractive price. Graeme was disappointed, especially because his prices were based on an hourly rate of £10, which he thought was quite reasonable. However, the competitor employed teenagers to do a good deal of the work and paid them little more than the minimum wage. This was quite different from Graeme's pricing policy. Even simple weeding was being priced at £10 per hour, making it impossible to compete with the other service.

ACTIVITIES

TASK 1

Graeme received an enquiry to carry out weeding, which he estimated would take 2 hrs and 45 minutes, and also create a rockery, which he estimated would take 4 hours.

1. Calculate the amount Graeme would charge for the work.
2. Explain why the competing firm would probably charge less for this work.
3. Suggest a likely price and explain how you arrived at this price.

TASK 2

Some customers may be prepared to pay more for a service. Discuss with a partner what Graeme could offer that would attract customers despite his higher price. **This may be shared in class discussion later.**

TASK 3

Look at the following list of places a product could be sold in or from.

- Internet
- Retail shop
- Market stall

Suggest a product which would be well suited to be sold in or from each place.

State why you believe it would be a suitable place.

Use a different example of a product for each place.

TASK 4

You have been asked to launch an advertising campaign for Graeme's gardening business. With a partner:

- Create an advertising poster to be displayed at key locations.
- Include an advertising logo for the product.
- Decide on where you will advertise the product.

MAKE THE LINK

- We learn about creating artistic images for advertising in **Art & Design**.
- We learn about plant cultivation in **Biology**.
- We learn about laws, such as The Minimum Wage Act, in **Modern Studies**.
- We learn how to perform calculations in **Maths**.

DID YOU KNOW?

Just like a plant or other living thing, products have a **life cycle**. A product will have an **introduction** stage when it is new on the market. Any mistakes at this stage could lead to the product failing to capture the interest of consumers. The popularity of the product will increase during the **growth** and **maturity** stages but eventually the product will go into **decline** and may be **withdrawn** from the market. However, action can be taken to **extend** the life of a product, meaning it is on the market for a very long time. Can you think of any products that have been on the market for many years?

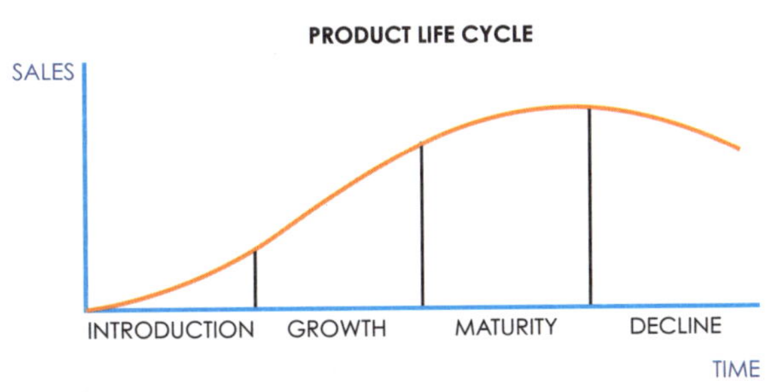

OUR EVERYDAY LIVES

We often see bargain range products in supermarkets. These are aimed at a market segment with a lower income including students and families on a budget. These products are priced with the market segment in mind. Supermarkets also sell premium ranges, aimed at a market segment with more to spend.

INTERDISCIPLINARY PROJECT

MARKETING 2 – THE MARKETING MIX

Around the UK Holidays is a company organising short trips from Scottish cities to locations around the British Isles. The company calculates the price it charges by adding together the various elements that are to be included in the trip. To this they add 10% commission, which is charged by the travel agent, then they add 20% VAT, a tax that is paid to the government.

The image shows an extract from a spreadsheet the company uses to calculate the cost to customers for the popular London trip.

◇	A	B	
1	**Around the UK Holidays**		
2			
3	**Package 1 Lively London**		
4			
5	Return train journey	£	45·00
6	3 nights in 3-star hotel	£	120·00
7	3 breakfasts	£	21·00
8	Theatre ticket	£	25·00
9	**Total cost**	**£**	**211·00**
10	Agent commission	£	21·10
11	**Total including commission**	**£**	**232·10**
12	VAT	£	46·42
13	**Total to pay**	**£**	**278·52**

Open a spreadsheet and key in the data shown in the image. Cells B9, B11 and B13 should contain formulae.
Now key in three other packages:

Package 2 is to Historic York.

- The details for this trip should start at cell A20.
- The return train journey is £30, two nights in a 2-star hotel cost £60, two breakfasts cost £10 and a city tour costs £24.

Package 3 is to Beautiful Bath.

- The details for this trip should start at cell D3.
- The return train journey is £80, three nights in a 4-star hotel cost £150, three breakfasts cost £18 and an excursion to Bristol costs £70.

Package 4 is to Cool Cardiff.

- The details for this trip should start at cell D20.
- The return train journey is £90, two nights in a 3-star hotel cost £70, two breakfasts cost £16 and a tour of the Millennium Stadium costs £17.

The formulae used in the Lively London package should be included for each of the other packages.

MAKE THE LINK

- In **Maths** and other subjects we perform calculations, both mentally and with the aid of a computer or calculator.

ACTIVITIES

TASK 1

Around the UK Holidays offers a discount of 5% **before VAT and agent commission is added** if the customer books early. Recalculate the cost of each trip if an early booking is made. You will have to insert two new rows for Early booking discount and Cost if booked early. Do this for each package.

◇	A	B
1	**Around the UK Holidays**	
2		
3	**Package 1 Lively London**	
4		
5	Return train journey	£ 45·00
6	3 nights in 3-star hotel	£ 120·00
7	3 breakfasts	£ 21·00
8	Theatre ticket	£ 25·00
9	**Total cost**	**£ 211·00**
10	Early booking discount	
11	**Cost if booked early**	

TASK 2

The rise in the rate of VAT has made these trips more expensive for customers. If the rate rose even further, say to 22%, the trips would be even more expensive. Change the rate on your spreadsheet to 22% to see how much more expensive the trips would be.

TASK 3

Discuss with a partner the likely effect if another company set up in competition with Around the UK Holidays. In particular, do you think they would have to rethink their pricing policy? If so, why?

TASK 4

Some products are thought of as **prestige** products. The price is purposely high to convey the message to consumers that this is a quality product.

Make a list of products which are priced expensively to make them seem exclusive.

MY LEARNING CHECKLIST

Put a tick in the column to show how you think you got on with each statement.
Green means you got on really well with your learning in this area.
Amber means you did well with your learning.
Red means you need to do a bit of work on your learning.

	Good to go!	Getting there	Help needed
1. ***I understand why products are advertised.***	○	○	○
2. ***I understand the benefit of a spreadsheet for performing calculations.***	○	○	○
3. ***I understand that a competitor offering the same product can result in a price war.***	○	○	○
4. ***I understand that companies sometimes offer a discount to encourage customers to pay early.***	○	○	○
5. ***I understand that some products are given a high price to make them seem exclusive.***	○	○	○

OPERATIONS 1 – MAKING YOUR PRODUCT

A company's **product** can be:

- a **good** – something we can touch and see, e.g. a table
- a **service** – something which we cannot touch or see, e.g. legal advice.

No matter whether the business sells a good or a service, the popularity of its product will, to a large extent, depend on the product's **inputs**. We cannot expect a quality end product – or **output** – if what is put into the product is of low quality.

TOP TIP

Quality standards of manufacturers may mean that a product does not reach completion if a defect is found during the process. However, often the product will be sent for reworking and not simply scrapped.

EXAMPLE

Invite Me! received sixteen complaints in a two-month period. This, it was agreed, was too high and action would have to be taken. Some complaints involved:

- poor quality cards
- spelling errors in invitations
- fading ink in some invitations
- late delivery.

It was concluded that the reason for disappointment in the standard of the **output** was the standard of the inputs.

ACTIVITIES

TASK 1

Look at the list of end products. Discuss with a partner the raw materials that go into the product and how the raw materials could contribute to the product being of poor quality.

- bread rolls
- training shoes
- shampoo
- paint
- vegetable soup
- school blazer.

TASK 2

One input in any production process is labour. If workers are not trained to do their job, the consequences can be serious. Suggest three negative consequences of not training workers properly.

TASK 3

In recent times, machines have replaced workers to quite an extent in production processes. Look at the following jobs and suggest a machine or other piece of equipment which has – at least in part – replaced the need for a worker:

- typist
- factory worker
- checkout operator
- baker.

Can you think of any other workers who have been replaced (or reduced) by machines?

TASK 4

Suggest actions producers can take to keep quality of products high.

MAKE THE LINK

- We learn about changes to work processes over the ages in History and Modern Studies.
- We learn about the appropriate use of language in **English**.

DID YOU KNOW?

Many jobs that are now done using machines used to be done by hand. One example of this is transport. In years gone by, a bus conductor would have sold tickets to passengers but nowadays advanced technology allows a driver to issue tickets as the passenger boards the bus. This is a big saving for the bus company. Despite the increased cost of technology, only one wage is paid per bus instead of two. We describe this as being more 'capital intensive' and less 'labour intensive'.

OUR EVERYDAY LIVES

We often see a quality symbol displayed on a product. This reassures the consumer of the product's quality and that it is safe to use. One example of this is the Lion Brand, which can be seen on eggs. It tells the consumer that the egg is of a good standard and safe to eat.
With a partner, carry out some research to find out about other quality symbols.

INTERDISCIPLINARY PROJECT

OPERATIONS 1 – MAKING YOUR PRODUCT

Producers aim to speed up their production process. By doing this, they can produce more items in a shorter time, leading to higher sales and profit.

This project aims to show how, by organising the workforce so that each worker carries out only one task, production can be increased.

To carry out this project, the class will have to be divided into groups of four or five. You will need coloured card, scissors, stencils, glue sticks and glitter.

You will have to agree as a class what will be made. An obvious product is some kind of greetings card but, as a class, you may come up with another idea. It is important that the class agrees on what the finished product will look like.

Half of the teams will make as many items as possible in a given time. It is essential that each member of these teams makes the items from start to finish on their own.

The other teams will also make as many items as possible in the same length of time. However, in these teams each team member will be given a task, for example one person will cut the card, one will fold, and so on. You can have more than one team member on the same task if you think it is a task that takes a bit longer than the others.

It might also be a good idea to have one or two students check that the quality of the items meets an acceptable standard.

When time is up, count the number of items made by each group. Which groups have the highest output?

MAKE THE LINK

- In History (and other subjects) we learn about the changes in production methods over time.

ACTIVITIES

TASK 1

When the making of a product is divided into different tasks, we call it 'division of labour'. Discuss within your group why you think your total output was higher/lower than some of the other groups. Your thoughts could be used in a class discussion.

TASK 2

Think about any disadvantages there may be of workers only doing one part of a job, rather than making something from start to finish. Discuss this in your group. Again, this can be used in class discussion.

TASK 3

1. Discuss in your group why it may be that different pieces of expensive machinery are used in a factory where division of labour is used.
2. Also discuss in your group likely costs that a factory would have to pay if they introduced machinery into their production process.

TASK 4

Sunny seats is a company producing garden chairs. In 2010, 95 000 chairs were produced. Since introducing division of labour, their production has risen by 19% in 2011. The company has estimated that their production will rise by a further 12% in 2012 because they are introducing machinery. They will therefore be more **capital intensive** and less **labour intensive**.

1. Calculate the number of chairs produced in 2011.
2. Calculate the estimated number of chairs in 2012.

MY LEARNING CHECKLIST

Put a tick in the column to show how you think you got on with each statement.
Green means you got on really well with your learning in this area.
Amber means you did well with your learning.
Red means you need to do a bit of work on your learning.

	Good to go!	Getting there	Help needed
1. *I understand the benefits of division of labour.*	○	○	○
2. *I know that there are some disadvantages of division of labour.*	○	○	○
3. *I understand the difference between being labour intensive and capital intensive.*	○	○	○
4. *I understand that there are costs associated with introducing machinery into a production process.*	○	○	○
5. *I understand how to calculate a rise in production in percentage terms.*	○	○	○

OPERATIONS 2 – CHOOSING THE METHOD OF PRODUCTION

Think of a cake made for a certain person, perhaps to celebrate an occasion. Think of a cake made by a bakery for sale on a certain day.

Think again of a cake – but this time one of a large number, possibly made by a well-known manufacturer such as Mr Kipling.

All of these products will be made in different ways, as described below:

EXAMPLE

Job production – My name is Neil McTavish. I am a specialist maker of cakes. Customers send me very precise instructions about what they want. In eighteen years of trading, I have never turned down a request. I have made a weather map cake for a retiring meteorologist, a cake in the shape of a hairdryer to celebrate the opening of a hairdressing salon and even a koala bear for a family emigrating to Australia. I charge my customers based on the materials used but also the time likely to be taken, which can be quite a few hours.	
Batch production – My name is Shona Stewart. I am a trained baker and work in a local bakery. With my co-workers, I make a range of baked goods. We start very early in the morning and bake items to be sold that day only. Experience tells us that demand for the various items will vary depending on the day and the time of year. For example, on the night before Christmas Eve we bake through the night because we know that customers will queue out the door that day.	
Flow production – My name is Eddie Lee. I work as a supervisor for a large food manufacturer on a production line. My job is to ensure that the line is moving along well and that the high standards expected by the company are maintained. The production line never stops and every cake made is identical. When my shift ends, another supervisor takes over.	

ACTIVITIES

TASK 1

1. Make a list of items that might typically be made using **job** production.
2. Discuss with a partner why a product made in this way will probably mean a high price tag.
3. Discuss with your partner why customers may like products made in this way.

TASK 2

1. Make a list of items that might typically be made using **batch** production.
2. Making products in this way will probably cost less than making them using job production. Discuss with a partner why this is true.
3. Discuss with your partner why batch production may be suitable for a business such as a bakery.

TASK 3

1. With a partner, carry out research to find out the names of food manufacturers in Scotland likely to use **flow** production.
2. Discuss with your partner why producing in this way is likely to bring down costs.

TASK 4

Some businesses use a practice called 'outsourcing'. For example, the bakery could make the mincemeat used for their mincemeat tarts in the bakery but instead they buy in the mincemeat from another company.

1. Discuss with your partner reasons why a business may choose to outsource.
2. Can you think of any problems which may be associated with outsourcing?

TOP TIP

A company with a large output is likely to be able to keep its production costs per item low. This is due to **economies of scale.** Division of labour is one example of an economy of scale. The high output of a large company makes division of labour worthwhile.

MAKE THE LINK

- We learn about the importance of keeping to strict procedures, including hygiene, in food preparation in **Home Economics**.
- We learn about changes to work processes in **History** and **Modern Studies**.

DID YOU KNOW?

Although division of labour can speed up production, it can deskill workers. This means they only perform a sub-task, depriving them of job satisfaction. The result can be loss of morale and lead to a dissatisfied workforce.

OUR EVERYDAY LIVES

Services are well suited to job production. For example, wedding planners are very popular nowadays. The wedding planner will undertake the entire wedding, from invitations and venue to photographs and clothing for the bridal party. No two weddings will be exactly the same and they will be planned from start to finish exactly to the specification of the bride and groom. The happy couple will feel their special day is unique but, unsurprisingly, the price will be high. Other important events can be planned by professionals. Think of the kind of events suited to this service.

INTERDISCIPLINARY PROJECT

OPERATIONS 2 – CHOOSING THE METHOD OF PRODUCTION

Different products are suited to different methods of production. Although the production rate will probably rise if products are made using flow production rather than job production, the **profit margin** – the amount added to a product on top of the cost of making it – may be much higher on an item made by job production. After all, the product will be a one-off original design and the customer will be prepared to pay a high price for it.

This project involves writing an article for a business magazine. The project should be carried out in groups of three. All three of you will contribute to the article.

For the article:

- One of you will write between 100 and 200 words on **job production**.
- One of you will write between 100 and 200 words on **batch production**.
- One of you will write between 100 and 200 words on **flow production**.

Your contribution to the article should include a description of the type of production. You should also include any good or bad points about the type of production.

You should type up your own part of the article. When you have finished, read each other's work. You may suggest changes to what other members of your group have written to improve the article. It would be ideal if you could each put your part of the article onto a pen drive so that the article can be brought together into one document. You may even be able to use Microsoft Publisher to improve the look of your article.

Finally, between you, decide on a good title for your article and include your names at the end.

MAKE THE LINK

- In **English** we learn to write in an engaging way to grab the reader's attention. This skill transfers to any subject requiring us to write in a descriptive and interesting way.
- Many subjects require us to perform calculations, including **Science**, **Home Economics** and **CDT**.

ACTIVITIES

TASK 1

You are a designer of wedding dresses and use job production. In about thirty words, write an advertising feature stating why customers should buy your products.

TASK 2

1. Mandy Lennox knits speciality woollen items to the direct specification of her customers. No two items are ever the same. Mandy knits and sells about twelve items per month for an average price of £48. The average cost of producing an item is £18. Calculate the average profit made per item.
2. The term 'mark-up' describes the percentage added to the cost price to give the selling price. Calculate Mandy's mark-up if she makes a product for £18 and sells it for £48.

TASK 3

Some products are very labour intensive, meaning they require a lot of labour hours to make them. Some products are made automatically with few labour hours. Such an industry would be described as capital intensive.

Is Mandy's business labour or capital intensive? State why you believe this.

TASK 4

When a producer starts out in business, it is quite likely that they won't make a profit straightaway.

State why you think it might be hard to make a profit to begin with.

MY LEARNING CHECKLIST

Put a tick in the column to show how you think you got on with each statement.
Green means you got on really well with your learning in this area.
Amber means you did well with your learning.
Red means you need to do a bit of work on your learning.

	Good to go!	Getting there	Help needed
1. ***I understand the different methods of production.***	○	○	○
2. ***I understand why products are suited to a particular method of production.***	○	○	○
3. ***I understand the meaning of the terms*** **profit margin** ***and*** **mark-up.**	○	○	○
4. ***I understand the terms*** **capital intensive** ***and*** **labour intensive.**	○	○	○
5. ***I know how to write in a way that keeps the reader interested.***	○	○	○

OPERATIONS 3 – QUALITY MATTERS

A producer or retailer failing to take quality seriously is unlikely to succeed. The consequences of allowing the quality of a product to slip can be serious, for example:

- Customers may complain and demand a refund.
- Customers may not return in the future.
- Customers are unlikely to recommend the product to others.
- The company may get a bad reputation.
- In the most extreme circumstances, customers may sue the company.

Case 1

Jeremy Holland treated his family to a meal at Hardy's, a popular restaurant in a nearby town. The service was slow and, when the food arrived, it was cold and poorly presented.

Case 2

Susan Brockman bought an action doll from a local toyshop for her young nephew. On arrival home, Susan decided to examine the doll carefully before posting it. She was shocked to find that the head of the doll was held on by staples, several of which were sticking out of the doll.

Case 3

Mark Elder had his roof tiles replaced by a company called Quality Roofers. During the next spell of heavy rain it became clear that the job was sub-standard as damp patches began to appear on Mark's ceiling. Despite several telephone calls and a strongly worded letter, the company has not responded to Mark's complaint.

ACTIVITIES

TASK 1

With a partner, consider each of the cases outlined on page 102. Decide together on advice you would give each consumer on action they should take.

TASK 2

Lucy Wilkins has a joint bank account with her partner, Raymond Barker, which they use to pay their household bills. £500 is transferred each month from Lucy's personal bank account into the joint account. Recently, Raymond has paid additional bills, including his gym membership, from the joint account, meaning that more was drawn out than paid in. Without consulting Lucy, the bank took money from her personal account to clear the debt in the joint account. Lucy was furious. She thinks the bank acted against the law.

Is this true? Carry out some research with a partner to find out. Hint: http://www.cas.org.uk may help you.

TASK 3

You instructed a local firm of decorators, Ace Decorating, to paint your kitchen pale green while you were away on holiday. When you returned you found that the kitchen was painted blue. You have a copy of the quotation from the company, clearly stating that the kitchen would be painted green. You also have a copy of your acceptance of the quotation.

Write a letter to Ace Decorating, which sets out your complaint. Include all of the facts and ask for the mistake to be put right. Remember to use language that makes the position clear.

TASK 4

You have been asked to prepare a presentation on points to remember when preparing and storing food. In a PowerPoint presentation, give details of four or five important points and why they are important. The website http://www.nhs.uk/livewell/homehygiene/pages/how-to-store-food-safely.aspx will be useful for carrying out this task.

MAKE THE LINK

- We learn about the importance of using appropriate language in **English**.
- We learn about taking care when preparing and storing food in **Home Economics**.
- We learn about the importance of being protected by laws in **Modern Studies**.

DID YOU KNOW?

We have all been given gifts we don't like. It is commonly believed that a consumer is entitled to an exchange or refund, but that is not the case. Some retailers may offer an exchange or refund but, unless the item is faulty, the law does not state that the consumer is entitled to a refund or exchange. If you think you may wish to return an item, check out the retailer's policy. For example, they may offer an exchange but they may state that the item must be returned within twenty-eight days of purchase. However, this period is often extended in the run-up to Christmas. Why do you think that might be?

OUR EVERYDAY LIVES

You may be dismayed if the soles of a recently purchased pair of boots split after a walk in the Pentland Hills. However, the **Sale & Supply of Goods Act 1994** should be considered. An item sold must be 'fit for purpose' so if your boots were sold as 'fashion boots' and clearly were not designed for a hike in the hills, the boots could not be returned as faulty. Some retailers will exchange or refund a customer even if they are not legally obliged to. Why do you believe a retailer may do this?

INTERDISCIPLINARY PROJECT

OPERATIONS 3 – QUALITY MATTERS

We know that maintaining and improving the quality of products is an important factor for any organisation competing in the market. In fact, some organisations aim to exceed the expectations of their customers so that the customer returns and also tells others of their experience.

It would be interesting to find out the experiences of various individuals in relation to customer service. Decide on a range of people to ask about a time when they have been either satisfied or dissatisfied by a good or service they purchased. Choose about seven or eight people to ask, bearing in mind you may not receive a response from them all. Ideally, replies from four or five people would work very well.

- Write a letter explaining that you would like to gather examples of good or bad customer service and requesting details of experiences. Your letter should go to a range of people, based on age and gender.
- Once you have received your replies, read what they say. Do you see any pattern? For example, is there any difference in the experience of older and younger people?
- Based on the feedback, prepare a report – about 300 to 500 words. Your report should include an account of the various experiences but it should also include a conclusion. To come to a conclusion, you must consider the experiences and make a point about anything that occurs to you, for example, 'men seem to get better service than women'.
- It would be good if your report could appear in your school magazine or on the school website.

Tips:

- You can include responses from people at home, such as family or neighbours, in your article, or staff in school. You could also have a mixture of both.
- Make sure you ask the contributors if they mind being named in the article. If they want to stay anonymous, you must respect that.
- You may choose to work with a partner on the report, dividing the work equally. This is known as 'collaborating'.

MAKE THE LINK

- We learn how to write reports in **English**.

ACTIVITIES

TASK 1

A good-quality product depends to a large extent on a well-trained workforce. This does not only apply to new staff. Existing staff must also keep up-to-date with their training needs because of changes inside and outside of the organisation. Think about changes that could occur which would require an existing workforce to undergo training. Make a list of reasons for the training to take place.

TASK 2

Think about your experience in a restaurant or café (it could even be the school cafeteria). With a partner, make a list of points that you think would make the difference between your experience being good or bad.

Basement Bob's on the Up!

Local restaurant, Basement Bob's, has seen a big improvement in customer numbers since the beginning of this year. How have they managed to 'buck the trend' of restaurants losing customers during the recession? Well, it seems that they have hit upon the idea of 'lunchtime tasting'. They now offer a few selected dishes from their menu at lunchtime. Diners can enjoy two courses for a very attractive £9.40. The portions are smaller than in the evening, but otherwise the food and service is to the same high standard. As a result, it is almost impossible to get a table at lunchtime without booking. And it seems that diners, impressed by the lunchtime menu, are returning for the full menu in the evenings. Clearly, this local business in a basement is aiming for the top!

TASK 3

In the article in Task 2, the restaurant charges £9·40 for the special lunch.
The price is calculated by adding VAT of £1·40 to the price of £8·00. However, since this article was written, VAT has risen from 17·5% to 20%.

1. Calculate the new price of the meal with the new rate of VAT.
2. Can you think of any reasons why the restaurant may be disadvantaged by this increase in VAT?
3. Calculate the price charged to the customer if VAT changed to:
   a. 15%
   b. 18%
   c. 22%

MY LEARNING CHECKLIST

Put a tick in the column to show how you think you got on with each statement.
Green means you got on really well with your learning in this area.
Amber means you did well with your learning.
Red means you need to do a bit of work on your learning.

	Good to go!	Getting there	Help needed
1. *I understand the importance of maintaining and improving quality.*			
2. *I understand that laws protect customers with regard to quality they can expect.*			
3. *I understand that a recession may damage the success of a business.*			
4. *I understand about proper storage and service of food.*			
5. *I understand the link between staff training and good quality.*			

FINANCE 1 – FINANCIAL DOCUMENTS

Businesses are required to produce a range of financial documents. Various stakeholders will have an interest in seeing these documents. For example, shareholders in a company may wish to see the profits of the company before deciding whether to keep or sell their shares.

EXAMPLE

Before starting in business, Grant Reynolds took a course in basic accountancy. Grant learned about various important financial documents, including:

- Trading, profit and loss account – which shows the amount of profit or loss made by the business in an accounting period.
- Balance sheet – which shows the worth of the business in terms of what it owns and what it owes.

ACTIVITIES

TASK 1

Look at the following profit and loss account. Some figures are missing. Insert the missing figures.

Grant Reynolds Upholstery
Trading, profit and loss account for year ended 31.12.10

		£	£
Sales[1]			30 000
Less – Cost of sales[2]			20 000
	Gross profit[3]		
Expenses[4]			
Staff Wages		2000	
Rent		4000	
Electricity		1000	
	Net profit[5]		

Notes:
1. Income received from customers from sales of products.
2. The cost of buying in the stock sold during this year.
3. The amount left after taking cost of sales from sales.
4. Expenses that have to be paid other than stock.
5. Remaining sum after taking expenses from gross profit.

ACTIVITIES

TASK 2

Look at the following balance sheet. Some figures are missing. Insert the missing figures.

Grant Reynolds Upholstery
Balance sheet as at 31.12.10

	£	£
Fixed assets[1]		
Machines		10 000
Motor vans		15 000
Current assets[2]		
Amount in stock	11 000	
Bank	12 000	
Less – current liabilities[3](owed to suppliers/creditors)	6000	
Net current assets[4]		
Working capital[5]		
Finance		
Capital invested at start by owner		30 000
Net profit this year		12 000
		42 000

Notes:
1. Owned items the business expects to still have in one year.
2. Owned items the business will not still have in one year.
3. Amounts owed which are expected to be paid within one year.
4. Value of current assets once the current liabilities are deducted.
5. The worth of the business based on what's owned and owed.

Any thoughts on why this is called a 'balance' sheet?

MAKE THE LINK

- We use our numeracy skills in various subjects. How many subjects can you list where numeracy skills are important?

DID YOU KNOW?

The recession has opened up opportunities for companies offering short-term lending. Often people find they do not have enough money to last until the next payday. The moneylender will lend a relatively small amount, say £100, for a week or so. The interest rate is very high. However, at least these lenders are regulated and preferable to unregulated moneylenders who may charge even more.

OUR EVERYDAY LIVES

Being able to calculate 'money in' and 'money out' is a very important life skill. At school age it is important because it is inconvenient if pocket money or earnings from a part-time job run out before the end of the week. However, it becomes much more serious as a householder with several bills to pay. If we continue to live with more money going out than coming in, eventually we have a debt with which we may not be able to cope. Planning income and spending is vital to avoid debt becoming a problem.

INTERDISCIPLINARY PROJECT

FINANCE 1 – FINANCIAL DOCUMENTS

Accessing finance is vital for any new business, or indeed a more established business, wishing to expand. Often, this finance will be accessed through more than one source. For example, the owners may put some of their own savings into the business and also apply for a loan from a bank.

This project involves role-play – and writing a short play.

Maureen McCann, an experienced physiotherapist, has arranged an appointment with her bank manager, Sam Finlay. Maureen wants to apply for a loan of £6000 to match her own savings of £6000 that she is investing. However, Maureen will require a smaller loan if she is awarded a grant she has applied for. The money is needed to buy equipment for the physiotherapy business she wants to start up. Some money is also required to alter the premises she is leasing to suit her needs.

Maureen has decided to go into business for herself in response to a number of local people complaining that there is no physiotherapy available in a ten-mile radius, neither NHS nor private. An ex-colleague of Maureen's set up a business in a town twelve miles away and is doing very well. At present, the ex-colleague employs no staff and Maureen intends to do likewise.

Maureen has prepared a business plan to take with her to the interview.

You should work on your script with a partner, with one person being Maureen and the other being the bank manager. You should write, then rehearse your script to ensure that it runs to **five minutes.** Ideally, the play should be filmed but your teacher may just wish to see you perform it.

Tips – the bank manager may wish to know about:

- any previous experience Maureen has in business
- the amount of capital (money) she will invest herself
- how quickly Maureen thinks she could pay back the loan
- if Maureen intends to offer security on the loan, for example her house.

MAKE THE LINK

- We learn to write scripts and perform plays in **English** and **Drama** but we may also use these skills in other subjects.

ACTIVITIES

TASK 1

Make a list of costs and expenses that Maureen is likely to have to pay. Some costs will be 'one-off' when she starts her business, such as redecoration. Others will be continuing, for example electricity. Make separate lists for one-off and continuing costs and expenses.

TASK 2

Maureen will have to consider her costs when writing her price list. Discuss with a partner other factors she will take into account when setting her prices.

TASK 3

Maureen's ex-colleague has told her that he offers a 5% discount to any patients paying their accounts within seven days. He does this to encourage early payment so that he has enough money in the business to allow him to pay for bills and supplies of materials. He explained to Maureen that avoiding a cash flow problem in the business is very important.

- Calculate the discount patients would get if Maureen took this advice and the amount payable by each patient.
  1. Patient 1 = £28·80
  2. Patient 2 = £30·40
  3. Patient 3 = £112·20

TASK 4

Carry out some research (online or another source) to find out the kind of information that would be included in a business plan. Also find out reasons for preparing a business plan.

MY LEARNING CHECKLIST

Put a tick in the column to show how you think you got on with each statement.
Green means you got on really well with your learning in this area.
Amber means you did well with your learning.
Red means you need to do a bit of work on your learning.

		Good to go!	Getting there	Help needed
1.	*I understand the different sources of finance for a business, both long-term and short-term.*	○	○	○
2.	*I understand reasons for preparing business plans.*	○	○	○
3.	*I understand the importance of businesses having sufficient cash flow.*	○	○	○
4.	*I understand the difference between one-off costs and continuing costs and expenses.*	○	○	○
5.	*I understand what is taken into account when prices are set.*	○	○	○

FINANCE 2 – STAYING LIQUID

In business, the term 'liquidity' describes the amount of cash the business holds. A business may be worth a good deal if, for example, it owns a valuable building, but that building is of no use if an electricity bill must be paid immediately. Many businesses have failed because they did not have enough cash to pay what they owe.

One way of helping liquidity is to plan ahead. A good way of doing this is to complete a **Forecast Cash Budget**, a financial document designed to help an organisation plan its spending over a number of months. This helps identify times when liquidity may become a problem. Look at Grant Reynolds Upholstery Forecast cash budget. You can see that the amount in the business bank account in March is much lower than three months earlier. If this trend continues, the business bank account will fall to a negative figure, meaning the organisation will require an overdraft (short-term loan).

Grant Reynolds Upholstery
Forecast cash budget for January, February and March

	January	February	March
Opening balance	£18 000	£16 000	£17 000
Received from cash sales	9000	14 000	8000
Received from credit sales	11 000	8000	6000
	38 000	38 000	31 000
Less:			
Stock	15 000	14 000	17 000
Expenses (wages, fuel, rent)	7000	7000	7000
	22 000	21 000	24 000
Closing balance	16 000	17 000	7000

EXAMPLE

In the second year of trading, Grant Reynolds hit a few problems. His products were still popular and he received a high number of orders. However, his customers were taking too long to pay, which created difficulty for Grant, who had bills and wages to pay. When Grant was late paying his assistant for the third month in a row, the assistant left. Also, his fabric supplier declined to supply Grant because of his failure to pay within seven days of delivery. Grant was in the habit of holding a great deal of fabric in stock, much of which he did not use. These problems were added to by the high amount Grant was paying to various service providers, for example, internet services and electricity.

TOP TIP

First in first out is a good way of managing stock. It is best to use the oldest stock before new because it avoids the danger of stock being unused after its expiry date.

ACTIVITIES

TASK 1

With a partner, discuss how Grant could improve his liquidity.

TASK 2

Grant has been advised to hold a three-day sale bonanza to sell some items which have been ordered and not collected.

1. Discuss with a partner what Grant could do to attract customers to the sale. (This could be made into a PowerPoint presentation.)
2. Suggest what Grant should do in the future to at least reduce the problem caused by uncollected items.

TASK 3

A major competitor of Grant's is Regent Upholstery Services. Recently this firm moved from large premises in the centre of Glasgow to a smaller and more manageable modern building on the outskirts of the city. The company sold its city centre building to developers of luxury flats.

Suggest reasons why the company may have moved. Hint: one reason involves liquidity.

TASK 4

Read the following text then answer the questions:

An alternative to a business buying large items such as machinery or vehicles is leasing. The business will never own these items (also known as 'assets') but it does prevent a large sum of money leaving the business at one time. The fact that the asset will never be owned may not be of concern to the company, as often these assets are 'depreciating', meaning they lose value over time. The leasing company usually provides maintenance to the asset, which is another saving.

1. Why would leasing help a company's liquidity position?
2. Apart from helping its liquidity, why else would a company lease assets rather than buy them?
3. What does it mean if an asset is 'depreciating'?

MAKE THE LINK

- We learn about problems surrounding non-payment of debts in **Social Education**.
- We learn about industry relocating in **Geography**.

DID YOU KNOW?

Holding a small amount of stock improves a company's liquidity position. However, there are other reasons for keeping stock to a minimum. Storage costs can be very high and this can be kept down by reducing stock levels. Also, insurance companies will charge less in premiums if a company can show that it does not hold excessive amounts of stock because less would be lost in a fire.

Can you think of any other events that would lead to a loss of stock?

OUR EVERYDAY LIVES

It is quite common for a business to have an overdraft facility. This means that if the business has a short-term liquidity problem, the bank will lend the business money over this period. When the business has an improved liquidity position, for example when customers pay, it can pay off the overdraft. Useful as this is, it comes at a price. Overdraft interest tends to be relatively high. Nevertheless, the alternative of having a liquidity problem can be very serious.

INTERDISCIPLINARY PROJECT

FINANCE 2 – STAYING LIQUID

We have learned about the importance of **cash flow** (or **liquidity**). Read the following account of a business with a serious cash flow problem. With a partner, draw up an action plan to help the business out of this situation. The action plan could be done on PowerPoint and shown to your class when finished.

It could include the following:

- The present situation the partners are in.
- What they could do to improve the situation.
- The likely result of the action taken.

EXAMPLE

Ken Adams and Martin Braithwaite are equal partners in Join Us, a joinery business in a Highland town. They have encountered difficulty because of a cash flow problem. They find themselves unable to pay their suppliers for wood and other materials. They cannot pay their electricity bill for their workshop. Also, the rent of the workshop is due soon and they do not have enough money to pay it.

Ken and Martin's problem has arisen for various reasons. They have a small shop at the front of the workshop where they stock a variety of tools. The shop is well stocked but they get very few customers. They only started the shop to fill some of the space in the workshop, which is very large. Much of the workshop is filled with machinery they never use.

However, Ken and Martin's main problem is customer payment. They sometimes have to wait two or three months for payment. Ken commented that he wishes their suppliers were as patient, as they require payment within one week of supplying Ken and Martin.

MAKE THE LINK

- We learn about the best ways to borrow money in **Social Education**.

ACTIVITIES

TASK 1

Some businesses charge customers a 'late payment penalty'. This can push up the costs and expenses in a business considerably. Calculate the extra Join Us would have to pay on the following payments if they pay late.

Supplier	Sum owed	Late payment penalty
Power 2U Energy Company	£910·00	2·5%
Fast Material Supplies	£1250·00	3% on first £1000, remainder 5%

TASK 2

Many businesses arrange bank overdrafts (short-term loans) from their banks to see them over periods when they have cash flow problems. Discuss with a partner whether Ken and Martin would be better to arrange an overdraft or pay the penalty charged by suppliers for late payment. What would Ken and Martin have to calculate before making a decision?

TASK 3

Businesses and private individuals alike use credit cards. They are a convenient way of paying for something without money leaving your bank account straight away. The credit card company sends an account at the end of the month showing how much the business (or person) owes. They also show a 'minimum payment' which the credit card holder must pay. If, however, the credit card holder does not pay the whole of the amount owed (the amount outstanding) a high rate of interest must be paid.

With a partner, carry out some research online to find out current rates of interest charged on credit cards. Compare the rates to see the best deal currently available.

MY LEARNING CHECKLIST

Put a tick in the column to show how you think you got on with each statement.
Green means you got on really well with your learning in this area.
Amber means you did well with your learning.
Red means you need to do a bit of work on your learning.

	Good to go!	Getting there	Help needed
1. I understand actions that can be taken to reduce cash flow problems.	○	○	○
2. I understand the consequences of late payment.	○	○	○
3. I understand the convenience (but also the danger) of paying by credit card.	○	○	○
4. I understand what 'minimum payment' means on a credit card statement.	○	○	○
5. I understand tactics used to persuade customers to pay early.	○	○	○

FINANCE 3 – RATIOS

We have learned about financial documents. They are important – and very useful. However, understanding ratios is a way of making the information in these documents even more useful.

Look again at Grant's trading, profit and loss account (page 104). We know that his gross profit is £10 000 – but is that good or bad? Could his gross profit have been better? Has he done very well to achieve this figure? We can only make these judgements if we compare Grant's gross profit with something else. This could be his gross profit in previous years, if this was not his first year of trading. The figure could also be compared with a similar-sized company's gross profit.

It would be interesting to note how much of Grant's sales end up as gross profit. £10 000 may seem quite impressive – but if Grant had a sales figure of, say, £100 000, this figure begins to look less impressive, as only 10% of his sales ends up as gross profit. This means for every £1 of sales, only 10 pence in gross profit is made.

Grant uses the following formula to calculate his **gross profit to sales percentage ratio**.

$$\frac{\text{GP}}{\text{sales}} \times 100 = \frac{10\,000}{30\,000} \times 100 = 33{\cdot}3\%$$

This means for every £1 of sales, 33 pence of **gross profit** is made.

Once Grant has taken his **expenses** from his gross profit, he will have his **net profit**. Grant can also use a ratio to calculate his **net profit to sales percentage ratio**.

$$\frac{\text{NP}}{\text{sales}} \times 100 = \frac{3000}{30\,000} \times 100 = 10\%$$

This means for every £1 of sales, 10 pence of **net profit** is made.

ACTIVITIES

TASK 1

Using the following financial information, calculate the **gross profit to sales percentage ratios** and **net profit to sales percentage ratios** for companies A, B and C.

Company	Sales	Gross profit	Net profit
A	£28 000	£14 000	£7000
B	£36 000	£6000	£2000
C	£117 000	£90 000	£60 000

Which company has done best and worst in terms of GP to sales and NP to sales?

Look again at Grant's balance sheet (page 105). Grant can use the information in this document to measure his liquidity. Grant's business is worth

(TASK 1 CONTINUED)

£42 000 – but does that mean he can pay his bills? Grant can be reassured about his liquidity if:

- He has twice as much in **current assets** as **current liabilities** – 2 : 1 – this is **the current ratio**.

$$\frac{\text{CA}}{\text{CL}}$$

He has as much in current assets **less stock** as current liabilities – 1 : 1 – this is **the acid test ratio**.

$$\frac{\text{CA} - \text{STOCK}}{\text{CL}}$$

Grant's current ratio = 23 000 : 6000 = 3·8 : 1

This means Grant has £3·80 of current assets to cover each £1 of debt.

Grant's acid test ratio = 12 000 : 6000 = 2 : 1

This means Grant has £2·00 of liquid assets to cover each £1 of debt.

Grant has no problem with his liquidity.

TASK 2

Using the following financial information, calculate the **current ratios** and **acid test ratios** for companies A, B and C.

Company	Total current assets	Stock	Current liabilities
A	£50 000	£30 000	£25 000
B	£36 000	£20 000	£16 000
C	£150 000	£50 000	£70 000

Comment on each company's liquidity position considering both ratios.

Grant invested £30 000 in the business. Grant has earned a return on this investment as he achieved a **profit** of £12 000 during his first year of trading. However, Grant could have put his £30 000 into a savings account in a bank or building society where he would have earned a return. This return would be called **interest** rather than **profit**.

Anyone deciding on whether to invest in a business would be wise to look at the balance sheet to see how much profit has been earned in the past on an investment. There is a ratio which calculates this so that it is easy to compare the return on the investment with an alternative investment. This is called **return on capital employed**.

$$\frac{\text{NP}}{\text{capital invested at start}} \times 100 = \frac{12\,000}{30\,000} \times 100 = 40\%$$

TASK 3

Using the following financial information, calculate the **return on capital employed** for companies A, B and C.

Company	Total investment	Net profit
A	£60 000	£6000
B	£44 000	£19 800
C	£150 000	£25 000

Which investment offers the best return?

MAKE THE LINK

- Ratios are useful tools which help in decision-making. In all of our subjects we use a range of tools which help us to make decisions. One example is the sources we use in subjects such as **History**.

DID YOU KNOW?

A businessperson earning a return on capital of say 40% may be quite happy. However, while putting the money in a savings account would not earn as good a return, the businessperson may have had to give up another job to work full-time in the business. The salary they would have earned in their previous job must be considered when a decision is being made.

OUR EVERYDAY LIVES

In a shop, we may see a sign offering a 5% or 10% discount on an item. We may also see the same item in another shop. However, if we are unable to calculate the discount, we cannot make a good decision on which shop to buy the product from. Often a sign may state 'Take 20% off all price tags in store today'. This may seem attractive if we are buying a shirt with an original price of say £20·00. However, if the shop next door is offering the shirt for £15·00, would you know where to buy it?

INTERDISCIPLINARY PROJECT

FINANCE 3 – RATIOS

Understanding ratios is vital for decision-making. If we consider Ken and Martin's business, Join Us, the partners are in a much stronger position to make decisions if they use ratios. Look at the following future scenario.

Ken and Martin have been approached by Laurence Stirling, a local electrician. Laurence is known to Ken and Martin as a good tradesman. Laurence has asked Ken and Martin to consider taking him on as a third partner. Laurence is prepared to invest £20 000 in the business, which would mean they could afford to buy new equipment. This equipment, they estimate, would mean their profits could rise the following year by £26 000. However, any profits made would have to be split three ways as Laurence insists that the three would be equal partners, sharing profits equally.

If Laurence joins the business, it is estimated that the profit in the following year will be £96 000 but without Laurence's investment the profit will only be £70 000. Profits in the years to follow would be expected to be higher with Laurence's input, although there are no certainties.

You will take the position of Ken, who thinks they should go forward with the proposition to take Laurence on. Your partner will take the position of Martin, who is against the plan. As Ken, write down all the reasons for accepting Laurence's offer. Your partner, as Martin, will write down his/her reasoning. Who made the more convincing case? Should Laurence's offer be accepted?

MAKE THE LINK

- We learn about algebra in **Maths**.
- We learn about accessing the right materials in various subjects, including **CDT** and **Home Economics**.

ACTIVITIES

TASK 1

Ken and Martin have been discussing their liquidity position. The table below shows examples of different businesses. Complete the missing figures. Remember, current assets should be at least double current liabilities and, if we take stock out of current assets, this figure should at least match the current liabilities figure.

Company name	Current assets	Value of stock	Current liabilities	Current ratio	Acid test ratio
Afton Associates	£6800	£3200	£2000	3·4 : 1	2·3 : 1
Burton Brothers	£6000	£3400	£3000		0·87 : 1
Carter & Co	£10 000	£4000	£6000	1·67 : 1	

TASK 2

Look at the position of the three companies in Task 1.

- How would you assess the liquidity position of the companies?
- What could they do to improve any areas of concern?

TASK 3

If Ken and Martin decide against taking on a partner, their profit next year is likely to be £70 000. This profit is **net profit**, meaning **expenses**, such as electricity and rent, will have been deducted. Their expenses are likely to be £14 000. Their sales figure is likely to be £210 000.

- Draw up a trading, profit and loss account for Ken and Martin.
- Calculate the **gross profit to sales % ratio**.
- Calculate the **net profit to sales % ratio**.

MY LEARNING CHECKLIST

Put a tick in the column to show how you think you got on with each statement.
Green means you got on really well with your learning in this area.
Amber means you did well with your learning.
Red means you need to do a bit of work on your learning.

	Good to go!	Getting there	Help needed
1. I understand the uses of the current ratio and the acid test ratio.	○	○	○
2. I understand the consequences of overstocking.	○	○	○
3. I understand possible advantages and disadvantages of taking on a partner.	○	○	○
4. I understand why gross profit percentage ratio and net profit percentage ratio help with decision making.	○	○	○
5. I know how the cost of materials could be reduced.	○	○	○

THE EUROPEAN UNION

The UK has been part of the organisation we now know as the European Union since 1973. Many people are what we could call 'pro-Europe', believing that membership is of great benefit to UK citizens. Others could be described as 'Euro-sceptics', meaning that they are not as convinced by the arguments for EU membership.

- Trade within the EU is made much easier because there are no **barriers to trade**.
- The citizens from member states are free to move around the Union seeking work.
- Laws are made by the EU which all member states are obliged to adopt.
- The majority of EU member states use a **common currency** called the **euro**.

EXAMPLE

My name is Aleska Krol. I am a Polish national and come from a small town near Gdansk. I came to live in Scotland in 2007 so that I could improve my English. I work for a large cinema chain in Glasgow and, even though I am over-qualified for the job I do, my earnings are significantly higher than they would be in Poland.

My name is Elma Angus. I am trained in horticulture and for many years have nurtured small plants which I sell in farmers' markets across the central belt of Scotland. However, I have found it increasingly difficult to sell my products in recent times. A major competitor, I find, is the Netherlands. As a member of the EU, plants produced in the Netherlands and imported by the UK are not restricted. I accept that I am equally free to sell my plants in the Netherlands and other EU countries, but I only produce enough for the home market.

My name is Kevin Wishart. I travel in Europe frequently, both for business and pleasure. Although the UK does not use the common currency, I always keep some euros in my wallet for convenience.

ACTIVITIES

TASK 1

- Discuss with a partner ways in which organisations such as the cinema chain can benefit from employing workers like Aleska.
- A 'skills gap' is when a country has a shortage of workers skilled to do certain jobs. With a partner, carry out research to identify where a skills gap may exist in Scotland. Discuss with your partner different ways of solving this problem.

TASK 2

1. Make a list of reasons why businesses could benefit from the UK using the euro.
2. Make a list of possible problems for British business if the UK adopts the euro.

TASK 3

Find out which countries are in the EU. Choose a country that you would like to work in one day. Why have you chosen this country? Can you think of any problems that may arise from working in this country? Write a short report containing:

- some information about the country
- why you would choose that country
- possible problems that may arise.

TASK 4

Crombies of Edinburgh is a famous firm, well known for a variety of products but especially sausages. The company provides an online service and there is no reason why customers abroad cannot buy the fine foods the company has to offer.

- Access the company's website – http://www.sausages.co.uk.
- Choose three or four products from the online service. Calculate how much the product (in kg) would cost in euros – you will have to find out the current exchange rate for sterling to euros.

TOP TIP

Not all European countries are part of the European Union. Carry out some research to find out which European countries are outside the Union.

MAKE THE LINK

- We learn the skills we need to calculate an exchange rate in **Maths**.
- We learn about imports and exports in **Geography**.
- We learn how to write in report form in **English**.

DID YOU KNOW?

The UK was not the only member state to opt to stay out of the euro when it was introduced in 2002. Denmark and Sweden chose to stay with their own currencies. Like the UK, these Scandinavian countries were concerned that being part of a common currency would affect their economies adversely. Do you know the currencies of Denmark and Sweden? If not, take the time to find out!

OUR EVERYDAY LIVES

It is no surprise, when we go into a supermarket, to see a whole range of products especially for people from a certain country. Supermarkets know that they will be more profitable if they meet the needs of their customers and, as our country becomes more culturally diverse, supermarkets respond by catering for these cultural tastes. The next time you are in a supermarket, try to find products aimed at a particular culture or nationality. Take a note of the culture or nationality the supermarket is catering for.

INTERDISCIPLINARY PROJECT

THE EUROPEAN UNION

Elma Angus, the seller of plants, finds the unrestricted competition from the Netherlands to be difficult for her business. However, many UK businesses – large and small – find the ease with which they can trade inside the EU to be an advantage. Crombies of Edinburgh produce products that may well be popular across Europe.

This project requires you to work in a team of three or four. You have been asked by the Scottish Government to be part of the development of a new website called Scotland Rocks. The intention is to sell a range of Scottish foods to the rest of Europe. The site is specifically aimed at EU member states.

To begin with, the products will be aimed at:

- France
- Germany
- Spain
- Italy

Shedding the image of deep-fried everything will not be easy. However, Scotland has amazing produce, from soft fruit to salmon and oatcakes to offal – and lots besides!

Use the internet and other sources of information to find out about some great food products from Scottish producers. Finally, decide on five products to promote on the site. Between you, you have to write a paragraph about each product persuading international consumers to try the products.

MAKE THE LINK

- In **Home Economics**, we learn about the foods of Scotland.
- In **Modern Languages**, we learn about translating into different languages.
- In **Geography**, we learn about importing and exporting and trade barriers.

ACTIVITIES

TASK 1

You have also been asked to help with a message to be posted on the website for German, French, Italian and Spanish consumers. You have to translate the following message into each of the four languages:

We hope you try our excellent Scottish products.

If you need help with the translation, the modern languages department is a good source. Alternatively, there are translation sites online.

TASK 2

We know that there are no trade barriers within the EU. However, trade barriers do exist outside the EU. Shown below are two very different trade barriers. Find out how each trade barrier works and why it would be used.

1. Quota
2. Embargo

TASK 3

Suppose it had been decided to expand the Scotland Rocks website to include non-food products. Make a list of possible additions to the site.

TASK 4

Free movement of labour around the EU can be useful: for example, it can help to fill skills gaps. However, a large number of people settling in one area can bring problems. Discuss with a partner problems that may well arise when a large number of people settle in a relatively small area.

MY LEARNING CHECKLIST

Put a tick in the column to show how you think you got on with each statement.
Green means you got on really well with your learning in this area.
Amber means you did well with your learning.
Red means you need to do a bit of work on your learning.

	Good to go!	Getting there	Help needed
1. *I understand the benefit of free trade within the EU.*			
2. *I understand that free trade can bring problems.*			
3. *I understand that not all European Union member states use the euro.*			
4. *I understand reasons for and against using the euro.*			
5. *I understand that problems can arise when a large number of people settle in one area.*			

ANSWERS

BUSINESS IN THE ECONOMY

PAGE 9

Task 1

1. Answers could include any profit-making organisation, such as BP, Marks & Spencer or even a market stall.
2. Answers could include any organisation which is funded and run by any level of government, including NHS hospitals, state schools, public libraries or any emergency service.
3. Answers could include any organisation which exists for the benefit of a good cause and is funded by donations, such as Oxfam, Barnardo's or a cancer charity.

Task 2

1. The government collects income tax when above a certain amount is earned. The government collects VAT when (most) items are purchased.
2. Tax taken from pay is a tax on earnings, so income tax is a tax on earnings. Any tax added to the amount paid for a product is a tax on spending, so VAT is a tax on spending.

Task 3

1. Fire service

PAGE 11

Task 2

1. a. The government taxes citizens in a variety of ways, including income tax and VAT. This is used to fund services in the public sector.
   The government borrows to bridge the gap between finance raised through tax and public sector spending.
   b. Decisions on funding for an organisation like this will be made by government. However, the government will delegate (or devolve) decision-making, for example, to NHS Scotland.
2. a. Shareholders
   b. Superdrug, Semichem
3. a. Collection tins
   Sponsored events
   Corporate donations (businesses)
   TV appeals
   b. Any not-for-profit organisation such as a tennis club

PAGE 13

Task 1

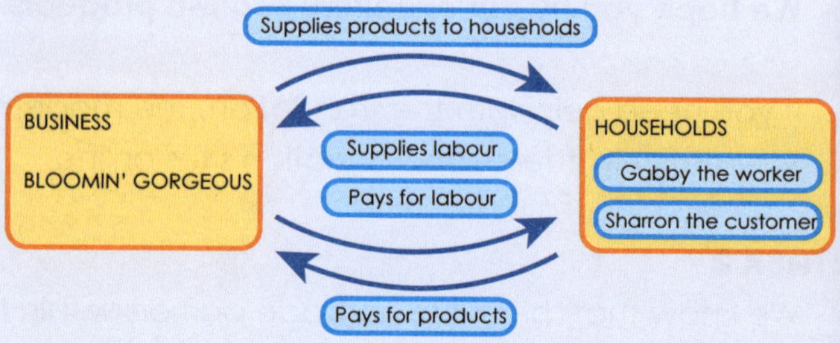

Task 2

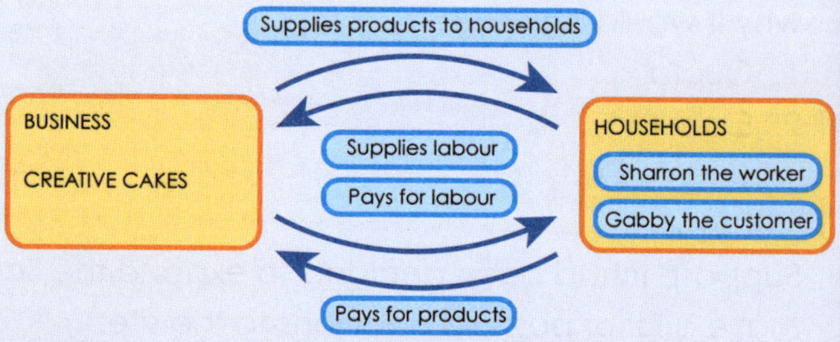

PAGE 15

Task 1

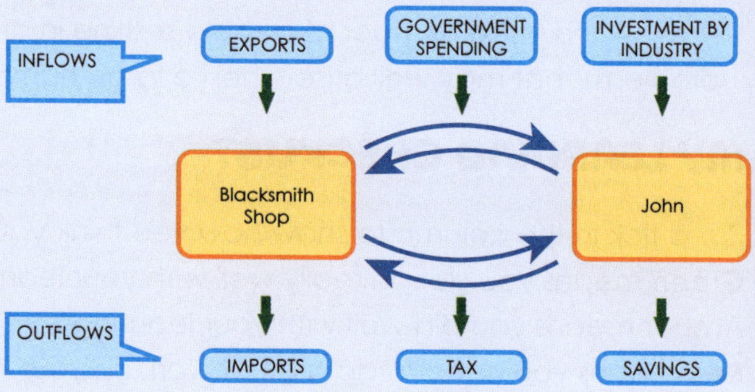

Task 2

1. Your answer may include some of the following:
   - health
   - education
   - emergency services
   - housing.
3. a. Your answer may include some of the following:
   - wedding
   - holidays
   - deposit for house
   - old age.
   b. People may believe the amount paid in interest is so small that is not worth it. For example, many people buy antiques or gold as investments believing they will become more valuable over time.

BUSINESS ORGANISATIONS

PAGE 17

Task 1

Gareth	Elaine
More investment meaning able to move to larger and better premises.	Splitting the profits may not provide enough for each partner to live on.
More diverse service offered which may attract more customers.	Disagreements may arise leading to problems for decision-making.
Fiona may have good business ideas to make service more popular.	Any mistakes made by Fiona may damage good reputation that has been built up.
If business fails leaving debt, Fiona would be liable for some of that debt.	Some existing customers may be put off if business is no longer a specialist male barber.

Task 2

1. Advantage for Fiona: She can be assured of receiving a salary without the risk of investing in the business.
   Disadvantage for Fiona: She will have no part in ultimate decisions, which could have led to greater business success (which might have benefited her).
2. Advantage for Gareth: If having a female stylist makes the business more popular, the profits will increase and he can keep the profits (only paying Fiona a salary).
   Disadvantage for Gareth: As an employee, Fiona will not put finance into the business, which means it will be harder for the business to expand.

Task 4

1. Your answer may include some of the following:
   - If popularity falls for one product, the popularity of other products can compensate.
   - The popularity of one product may transfer to other products.
   - Customers like being able to get more than one product in one place, e.g. a mother having her son's and daughter's hair done in one shop.
2. Your answer may include:
   - Sometimes staying focused on one product means customers see the business as a specialist company.
   - There can be a fear of 'over-extending', meaning everything is done less well.

PAGE 19

Task 2

1. a. Subway, Baguette Express
   b. Your answer may include some of the following:
   - Offer promotional deals, like buy one get one free, for a set period.
   - Offer new and exciting fillings not offered by competitors.
   - Advertise the business online, on TV, etc.
   - Offer a delivery service.
   - Offer 100% satisfaction guaranteed or your money back.
2. a. Your answer may include some of the following:
   - RBS
   - HSBC
   - Lloyds TSB Banking Group
   - Barclays.

   b. Your answer may include some of the following:
   - Apply for a grant from a body like Business Gateway.
   - Take on additional owners (partners or shareholders).
   - Existing owners could put in more finance.
   - Sell unused assets to reinvest.
3. a. Overhead costs can be high.
   The premises could be vandalised.
   b. Delivering to homes and businesses.
   From a mobile outlet, e.g. a van.
   In facilities such as an ice rink or an outdoor festival.

PAGE 21

Task 3

Names of partners
How much each will invest
How profits will be shared
If one or more partner will get a salary
How much notice of leaving partnership is required
Holiday entitlement

ANSWERS

Task 4

1. £24 954
2. Ray: £37 431; others (each): £18 715·50

PAGE 23

Task 2

1. a. • For advertising their product.
   - Raising finance by advertising other companies' products.
   - Customers like the convenience of online ordering.
   - It allows stakeholders to gain information about the business.

   b. Your answer may include some of the following:
   - contact details and location of business
   - information about key people in the business
   - range of products offered
   - special offers.
2. a. • Some partners may have more experience/contacts than others.
   - Some partners may have invested more capital than others.
   - Some partners may put more hours into the business than others.

   b. See above. Any of these conditions could change, e.g. hours worked may be reduced by a partner as they get older.
3. a. £24 471

   b. Ruth: £29 365·20; Bridget: £19 576·80

PAGE 25

Task 3

1. If a company could not buy on credit, it would be difficult to raise the finance at the start to buy stock. If they have time to sell at least some of the stock before they have to pay their suppliers, they will be better placed to pay their suppliers. If the company had to borrow to buy the stock, this would add more financial pressure to the company, possibly endangering their survival.
2. If a business is allowed to buy on credit, then cannot sell their stock, they may be unable to pay for the stock. This may cause serious problems for the business supplying the stock, especially if several of their customers fail to pay for stock purchased.

Task 4

1. 15%
2. Andrew: £54 000; Brian: £54 000; Charlotte: £45 000; David: £27 000

PAGE 27

Task 2

1. a. The investor knows that, although they could lose all the money they have invested in the business, they cannot lose anything else, e.g. personal assets such as their house.

   b. Generally, sole traders and partnerships do not have limited liability (although it is possible for a partnership to have limited liability).
2. a. The investor knows that, if they want to sell the shares and no authorised shareholder wishes to buy them, they may be stuck with the shares for some time.

   b. It can mean that the original shareholders in the company lose control of the company, which means the company has been taken over.
3. a. 50%

   b. Could include:

   Rise:
   - good profits reported for year
   - exciting new product being brought out
   - news about expansion into new towns

   Fall:
   - disagreements reported among directors
   - bad publicity about customer complaints
   - news about branch closures

PAGE 29

Task 3

1. £80
2. 20%
3. 28%

PAGE 31

Task 2

Occurrence causing share price change	Share price: up or down
New product found to be of poor quality	Down
Competing firm creates a new, popular product	Down
Large retailer decides to start stocking the product	Up
It is discovered that the company uses child labour in an Asian country	Down

Task 3

Issues may include the following:

- I would not invest in a company known to use child labour in developing countries as I believe this is morally wrong.
- I would not invest in a company investing in countries with poor human rights records because the investment in these countries helps them to carry on in this way.
- I would not invest in a company known to dispose of waste in a way which is harmful to the environment because I believe this practice is destroying the planet for future generations.

PAGE 33

Task 1

For all three questions, the answer is Louisa Drake.

Task 2

1. All twenty-six shareholders
2. The board of directors
3. All twenty-six shareholders

Task 3

For all three questions, the answer is both Louisa and George.

Task 4

1. She wants to float the business so that they can raise more finance.
2. She believes there is a danger that another company could buy enough shares in Chomp It to take control of the company.
3. Chomp It plc.

PAGE 35

Task 1

Your answer may include some of the following:

- awarding themselves bonuses considered to be too high
- profits disappointing
- disagreements known to occur between directors
- no strong plan for the future
- disappointing share dividends declared

Task 2

Type of finance	Advantages	Disadvantages
Instead of declaring high dividends, some profits could be reserved for investment in the future.	There are no high interest payments as there would be if funds were borrowed.	Shareholders may object to lower dividend, which could lower share price.
They could borrow from a financial institution or from private individuals.	The repayments are prearranged so won't rise if profits prove to be high.	In recent times, borrowed funds are much more difficult to access.

INFLUENCES ON BUSINESS

PAGE 37

Task 1

1. Internal
2. Internal
3. External
4. External
5. External
6. External

Task 2

1. They are likely to get higher bonus payments if the organisation does well.
2. They will get a better profit share if the organisation does well.
3. They get paid for what they sell to the organisation.
4. It receives tax from the organisation.
5. They get the benefit of the goods or services provided by the organisation.
6. They may object to some practices of the organisation, e.g. pollution caused by the organisation's activities.

PAGE 39

Task 1

1. Quiet times, possibly mid-week/during mornings, when paying customers are less likely to require the premises. This would mean John could give something back to the community without it having a serious impact on his profits.
2. John may feel loyalty to the area in which his business is located and may wish to help the area to keep a sense of community. Also, such a gesture will give John a good name and paying customers may therefore be more likely to book John's business.

ANSWERS

Task 2

Stakeholder	Internal/external	Influence
Suppliers	External	If they supply good products on time, this will have a good effect on the business.
Existing staff	Internal	If they treat customers politely, customers are likely to return and they will continue being employed by the business.
Government	External	Tax paid by business will help fund the public sector.

Task 3

(95 + 50 + 60 + 20 + 5 + 30) ÷ 130 = £2·00

PAGE 41

Task 1

Strategic	Tactical	Operational
Make food appeal to a wider range of consumers	Have outlets in more locations, e.g. petrol stations	Keep store in good order
	Sell more affordable products	Train staff in store
	Sell brand names, e.g. Heinz	

Task 2

1. Strategic
2. Tactical
3. Operational
4. Strategic
5. Tactical
6. Operational

Task 3

Do you think Simply Food products are too expensive?
The answers might include: some products are, all products are, products are good value for money.

Do you think the Simply Food range of products is wide enough?
The answers might include: there is not a wide enough range, the range of products could be wider.

Do you find Simply Food staff to be helpful and friendly?
The answers might include: some staff are, all staff are, generally they are not helpful and friendly.

Do you feel you get through the checkout quickly enough at Simply Food outlets?
The answers might include: always, usually, sometimes, never.

Task 4

1. 10
2. 40
3. 25%

PAGE 43

Task 1

1. Your answer may include some of the following:
   - Questionnaires could be sent out to local people.
   - Existing customers could be asked for their opinions.
   - A similar business could be looked at to see the kind of events it runs regularly.
   - Past enquiries could be looked at to find out what kind of events are requested.

2. John could put a lot of finance and time/effort into an event for which there is no enthusiasm, causing the event to make a loss. It may also take resources away from events which would have been more successful.

Task 2

1. This would lead to poor customer service. For example, customers would have to wait too long to be served or mistakes could be made by untrained staff. This would lead to complaints and a bad reputation for the business.

2. Over-staffing is expensive. The business would be paying too much in wages for staff who are not required.

Task 3

1. Strategic
2. Operational
3. Tactical
4. Tactical
5. Operational

Task 4

Meeting: All decision-makers in one room exchanging views instantly
Email: A time-efficient way of sending information to many people
Letter/memo: Some people still prefer information in 'hard copy'
Text: A good way of contacting many people, especially on the move
Telephone: Can get instant feedback if everyone not in same place
Online message board: Electronic way for everyone to interact

PAGE 45

Task 1

Tour	Month	Price in sterling	Price in euros	Price in US dollars
Highland Magic 7-day tour	April	Adult price £350	€402·50	$549·50
Highland Magic 7-day tour	April	Child price £250	€287·50	$392·50
Borders Beauty 10-day tour	June	Adult price £540	€621·00	$847·80
Borders Beauty 10-day tour	June	Child price £310	€356·50	$486·70

Task 2

1. They may have to take on more drivers.
   They may have to retrain drivers to take account of new rules.
2. They may have to either convert existing coaches or buy new coaches.
3. Journey times may have to be adjusted.
   Drivers may have to be retrained to take account of this rule.
   A device may have to be fitted in coaches to prevent speed being exceeded.

PAGE 47

Task 3

1. Internal
2. External
3. External
4. Internal
5. External

Task 4

Your answer may include some of the following:

- fire
- flood
- weather damage
- accidental damage.

ICT

PAGE 49

Task 1

=sum(D2:D9)

PAGE 51

Task 1

1. Your answer may include some of the following:
   - opening days/hours
   - how to get in touch
   - how to get there
   - schedule of forthcoming events
   - rates for hire
   - online booking facility
   - publicity about 'giving back to the area'
   - statement about aims and values of business.
2. Nowadays customers like contacting businesses online. Not having a website may stop customers from placing bookings.
   Information about the function suite can be found by potential customers outside the immediate area which may increase bookings substantially.

Task 2

1. (95 + 50 + 60 + 20 + 5 + 30 + 65) ÷ 130 = £2·50
2. (95 + 50 + 60 + 20 + 5 + 30 + 195) ÷ 130 = £3·50

ANSWERS

Task 3

1. Any task requiring a calculation can be done, including wages, invoices, costs, value of stock.
2. Any task requiring the storage and access of information can be done, including supplier, customer and staff details.
3. Any task requiring the keying in of information in an attractive way, including letters, memos, notices and reports.

Task 4

Costs include the financial cost of buying (and maintaining and upgrading) hardware and software, installing the equipment, closure while equipment is being installed, training staff.

PAGE 53

Task 1

Information	Electronic/not electronic
Details of similar businesses in the area	Electronic (online)
Delivery of questionnaires locally	Not electronic (on foot)
Looking for suitable premises to rent	Not electronic (newspaper)
Details about permission required to sell food	Electronic (online)

Task 2

Advantages:

- The internet allows information to be found from around the world which may make it more meaningful.
- The speed that information can be found makes investigating more time-efficient.

Disadvantages:

- It may not be possible to access the technology needed to gather information in this way.
- Too much information can be found online: It may take a long time to work through.

Task 3

- the kind of foods likely to be popular with customers
- the amount customers would be prepared to pay for products
- health and safety information for this kind of business
- information on environmental health and cleaning requirements

Task 4

1. To monitor whether his profits are increasing over time. If not, he may take steps to improve the situation.
2. Staff: To ensure they get a fair pay rise.
3. The government: To calculate the amount of tax due to be paid.
4. Staff records, such as absence and training undergone.
   Costs and expenses, such as rent and electricity.
   A record of accidents/hazards and when and how they were rectified.

PAGE 55

Task 1

Advantages:

- For some people at least, a letter can be more meaningful because of the effort involved compared to sending an email, e.g. a letter of thanks.
- A letter can reach everyone, no matter whether they have advanced technology or not.

Disadvantages:

- A letter can be a slow method of passing on information, especially if it is being posted ('snail mail').
- The cost involved in letter writing is relatively high, taking into account stationery costs and the cost of postage.

Task 2

1. The prices may have gone up, which would affect his costing.
   The supplier may no longer stock the products.
2. Company websites are usually updated very quickly with any changes.

Task 3

1. 87 – (87 × 20%) = £69·60
2. 87 – ((87 – 50) × 20%) = £79·60

Task 4

Customers may well feel they have been misled by the company. They may complain and the company may feel obliged to compensate customers who feel they have been misled. Otherwise, this could result in lost customers, who may also share their experience with others, leading to more lost custom.

PAGE 57

Task 1

1. They have used their brand name and transferred it to other products which are now received enthusiastically by consumers who have developed a trust in the company.

2. You may find it more convenient to buy online or you may find prices cheaper online.
3. Clothes are often better bought in a retail outlet because customers can try the item on to decide on suitability.
4. a. Ryanair, easyJet
   b. Direct Line, Churchill

Task 3

1. Nowadays there is consumer demand for online shopping. This is partly due to widespread computer ownership and internet access, and partly due to busy lifestyles, with internet shopping allowing consumers to avoid having to spend time in shops.
2. Customers may find products to be unsuitable when they arrive, leading to returns. They have to ensure that the website is secure but even secure websites can be targeted by hackers, leading to internet fraud.

Task 4

1. 10%
2. 17%
3. 20%

PAGE 59

Task 2

Telephone
Videophone
Webcam
Text message
Pager
Instant messaging
Email
Electronic notice board
Internet forum
Fax

Task 3

Advantages:

- Compared to other methods of advertising, pop-ups are an affordable method.
- It is possible to have the pop-up appear on a site likely to be popular with the intended target market.

Disadvantages:

- Pop-ups can be irritating, meaning the consumers a company is trying to attract may actually feel negatively towards the company.
- There are so many pop-ups online, the advert may simply get lost among all the other pop-ups.

Task 4

Your answer may include some of the following:

- They can text customers reminding them it is time for an MOT.
- They can text customers with offers, e.g. 10% off servicing next week.
- They can let customers know when their car is ready for collection.
- They can contact mechanics who are out on recovery jobs.

WHAT MAKES A BUSINESS EFFECTIVE?

PAGE 61

Task 1

1. Without an original idea, there would be no starting point. Ideas can be refined during the process but no process can start without an initial idea.
2. There would be disagreements. Each ideas person would want to take their idea forward.
3. Track down any resources needed for the project.
   Coordinate one task with another.
   Ensure that initial ideas are seen through to completion.
   Identify any problems which may arise.

Task 3

Setting	Team task
NHS hospital	Drive to improve ward hygiene
Restaurant	A special function such as a wedding
Supermarket	Change of store plan
Public library	Special event to encourage library usage, such as 'Reading Week'

Task 4

2. Different team members may have a different understanding of what the end result should be.
3. There may be too few or too many team members for the size of task.
4. There may be a lack of communication between team members.
5. There may be a poor mix of skills and talents, meaning some important tasks do not get done.

PAGE 65

Task 4

Some people may regard such symbols as inappropriate, especially if the organisation is seen as 'secular' (no religious input).
The organisation may have a strict uniform policy and the religious symbol may interfere with this.

ANSWERS

PAGE 67

Task 1

Your answer may include some of the following:

- Staff will feel hard-done-by if they lose their trip and consequently their motivation to work will not be as strong.
- The trip is an opportunity for staff to get to know each other, which may well improve relationships in the workplace, so benefiting the company.
- Being seen to be cancelling an annual trip is close to announcing that the company is not doing well – a dangerous signal to be putting out to various stakeholders.

Task 2

If an employee owns shares, they become a part owner of the organisation. The employee will see a direct link between their efforts and the success of the company, meaning they may work harder and have fewer days of absence.

Task 3

1. £1140
2. £57

PAGE 69

Task 3

1. Small businesses, unable to compete, may disappear, meaning local high streets have many empty shops.
   A great deal of traffic and consequent congestion may arise.
   If the organisation is a factory, fumes/smells may become a problem.
   The building can be a 'blot on the landscape'.
2. Resources for local organisations, such as educational resources for schools, can be supplied.
   Improve local amenities, such as improving an eyesore by planting trees or landscaping an area.
   Provide jobs specifically for local people.

PAGE 71

Task 3

28 pence

PEOPLE IN BUSINESS

PAGE 73

Task 1

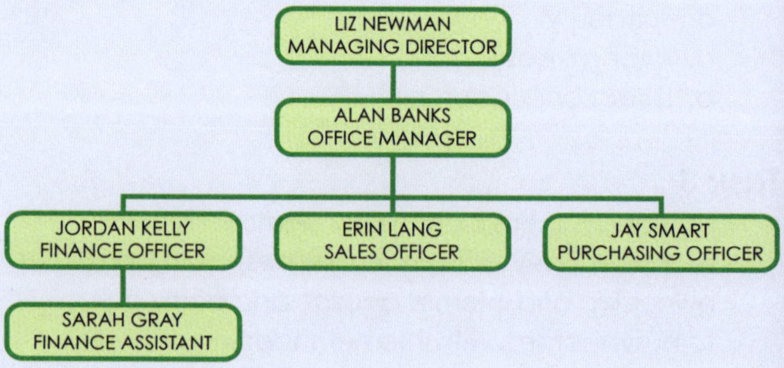

Task 2

1. Jordan, Erin and Jay
2. a. Jordan
   b. Alan
   c. Liz

Task 3

1. Sarah
2. Jordan, Erin and Jay

PAGE 75

Task 2

Your answer may include some of the following:

- newspapers, e.g. *Scotsman*, *Herald*
- employment agency
- recruitment website
- internal advert, e.g. staff noticeboard

Task 3

Your answer may include some of the following:

- Tell me about an important achievement in your life.
- Tell me about a time where you had to work towards a deadline and did you meet the deadline?
- Why do you want to work for this organisation?
- Where do you see yourself in two years' time?
- Tell me about a time when you worked effectively as a member of a team.

Task 4

Qualifications (certificates)
Reference from previous employer
Protecting Vulnerable Groups Scheme record

PAGE 77

Task 3

1. Interviewer interviewing a candidate for a job in the company
2. Conversation between two members of staff
3. Member of staff speaking to his/her line manager

PAGE 79

Task 1

Worse off by £1550 as he would be paid £19 000 plus £450 commission rather than £21 000

Task 2

£1,241·20

Task 3

Could include:

- Unhelpfulness of staff – addressed by training schemes to improve customer service
- Waiting times in queue at branch/on phone – addressed by employing more staff, promoting online banking
- Opening hours not long enough – addressed by extending opening hours in busiest branches, encouraging customers to use online or 24-hour telephone banking
- Unclear why charges have been made – addressed by making charges more transparent (clearer)
- Delays in receiving bank statements – addressed by automating the statement service to speed up process

PAGE 81

Task 3

Essentials:

- good level of literacy
- good communication skills

Desirables:

- previous experience in similar job
- knowledge of local area

Task 4

1. Yes
2. No
3. Yes
4. Yes
5. Yes
6. No

PAGE 83

Task 2

1. Your answer may include some of the following:
    - Test for problem-solving skills – Job: Any job in any aspect of management
    - Practical test – Job: A trainee chef
    - Audition – Job: Part in a play or any performance
    - Psychometric test: Job: Position likely to induce stress, e.g. medical training
2. Sometimes several candidates are invited to a training course and the most impressive candidate (or candidates) are offered a position with the organisation.
   Past performance. Particularly effective for internal candidates. Their 'track record' would be considered.

Task 3

It is a good way of finding out how the candidate performed in previous jobs, e.g. timekeeping, which gives an idea of how suitable they would be in the organisation.
Sometimes employees can exaggerate what they did in previous positions and a reference can set the record straight.
Some people are simply good at performing well in interviews, which can give a false impression of their suitability. A reference may give a clearer picture.

Task 4

Your answer may include some of the following:

- Hours/days worked
- Details of tasks to be carried out
- Temporary or permanent contract
- Holiday entitlement
- Pay and pay scale
- Notice required when leaving

MARKETING A BUSINESS

PAGE 85

Task 2

Questions may include:

- How often in a year do you send a greetings card?
- Please state the occasions on which you would send a greetings card.
- Have you ever had difficulty when trying to purchase a card for an occasion?
  Yes/No
- If you have answered Yes above, which occasion have you had difficulty buying a card for?
- Do you send traditional or electronic greetings cards? Traditional/Electronic/Both
- Approximately how much would you expect to pay for a greetings card?

Task 4

Could be:

Segmented by:	Groups
Level of earnings	Under £10 000 per year, £10 000–£30 000 per year, over £30 000
Age	16–24, 25–40, 40–50, 50–60, over 60
Gender	Male, female
Ethnic group	White, Asian, Black, Other (state)

PAGE 87

Task 1

In marketing, it makes sense to know something about a typical consumer likely to buy a product: for example, a certain type of face cream may be typically purchased by a woman in a certain age group, earning level and even a particular area of the country. Profiling will make it possible to target this consumer through an advertising campaign.

Task 3

1. *A League of Their Own, Soccer Saturday*
2. *Sonic the Hedgehog*
3. *T4* (Channel 4)
4. *Dancing on Ice*

Task 4

Italian community – cold meats such as salami, various pasta
Indian community – Indian herbs and spices, naan bread, samosas

PAGE 89

Task 1

1. £67·50
2. • They can keep their prices down by paying young workers at a lower rate to do some of the work.
   • The weeding could be done by a young worker and could be charged at £6 per hour. An experienced gardener (for the price of £10 per hour) could do the rockery. Thus, 6 × 2 hours 45 minutes = £16·50 + 10 × 4 hrs = £40. Total price: £56·50.

Task 2

'Satisfaction guaranteed' – promise to carry out work to exact requirements of customer
Online booking service for convenience of customer
Advice on plants and garden layout
'Organic pledge' – only organic weed killers used

Task 3

- Internet: books, CDs, appliances – no confusion with colour/sizing.
- Retail shop: clothing, fresh produce – opportunity to view in reality.
- Market stall: locally produced products, craft items - relatively small amount being sold makes this a good method.

PAGE 91

Task 1

◇	A	B
1	**Around the UK Holidays**	
2		
3	**Package 1 Lively London**	
4		
5	Return train journey	45
6	3 nights in 3 star hotel	120
7	3 breakfasts	21
8	Theatre ticket	25
9	**Total cost**	**=SUM(B5:B8)**
10	Early booking discount	=B9*5%
11	**Cost if booked early**	**=B9-B10**

Task 2

◇	A	B
1	**Around the UK Holidays**	
2		
3	**Package 1 Lively London**	
4		
5	Return train journey	45
6	3 nights in 3 star hotel	120
7	3 breakfasts	21
8	Theatre ticket	25
9	**Total cost**	**=SUM(B5:B8)**
10	Agent commission	=B9*10%
11	**Total including commission**	**=SUM(B9:B10)**
12	VAT	=B11*22%
13	**Total to pay**	**=SUM(B11:B12)**

Task 3

If another company set up in competition, the company would have to consider tactics to beat the competition, such as special offers or discounts for loyal customers. They may consider a competitive pricing policy, monitoring the price offered by the competition and matching or under-cutting that price. If they did not, customers may choose the competitor, leading to lack of customers for the company and possibly going out of business.

Task 4

- Rolex watches
- Designer clothing
- High-end cars, e.g. Porsche

BUSINESS OPERATIONS

PAGE 93

Task 1

Product	Raw materials	What could cause poor quality
Bread rolls	Flour	Moisture allowed into flour, meaning bread rolls don't rise
Training shoes	Leather	Inferior leather used causing shoes to crack
Shampoo	Oil/plant extracts	Ingredients used in wrong quantities
Paint	Binding agent	Wrong kind of binding agent used
Vegetable soup	Vegetable stock	Stock used beyond sell-by date
School blazer	Wool	Wool not hard-wearing enough for the type of garment

Task 2

- Workers feel they are not 'invested in', which can lower their morale and so their work rate.
- Errors can be made in the making of products, leading to a bad reputation for the company.
- The work rate can be low because workers are unsure about what they are doing.

Task 3

Typist: word-processor/computer
Factory worker: robot
Checkout operator: self-serve checkout
Baker: food-processor

Task 4

Your answer may include some of the following:

- good supervision
- random spot checks
- sharing ideas on good practice among workers.

PAGE 95

Task 2

- Workers may become demoralised through becoming deskilled (not being able to make something from start to end).
- Breaking tasks down lays the process open to stoppages if a worker trained to do a small (but vital) part of the task is absent from work.
- Striking can become more effective as it only requires workers performing one task to withdraw their labour to stop production.

Task 3

1. A piece of equipment may be required for every sub-task. A worker making a product from start to finish would need equipment for each task, whereas a worker only doing one thing only needs one particular piece of equipment.
2. Cost of equipment, installation cost, maintenance and upgrades, staff training.

Task 4

1. 113 050
2. 126 616

PAGE 97

Task 1

1. Your answer may include some of the following:
   - Designer clothing
   - Speciality cakes
   - Custom-built furniture
   - Landscaped garden
2. Tends to be labour intensive, adding to cost of production; unique (one-off) nature of product makes production cost high. Also, a customer buying a unique product is often prepared to pay a high price.

3. A unique product means that no one else will have the same product. Also, the product may be made exactly to the customer's needs, e.g. a cabinet to fit a particular space.

Task 2

1. Could include:
   - Bakery items such as rolls
   - Newspapers/magazines
   - Commemorative items, e.g. William and Kate mugs
   - Easter eggs
2. Unlike job production, items are not unique. For example, the same mould or pattern can be used multiple times. Also, the process is less labour intensive.
3. This type of production is suitable for making a set amount of items of a certain type, such as scones or cakes. A set amount is likely to be made by a bakery for sale that day.

Task 3

2. Mass-produced goods made in this way are capital rather than labour intensive, bringing down costs. Also, costs associated with marketing, heating, lighting, rent and so on are spread over a very large number of items produced.

Task 4

1. They may not have time/resources to make the input in-house.
   They may wish to get the expertise from another company.
2. They may not have control over the level of quality in the outsourced company.
   The company may charge a high price adding to production costs.

PAGE 99

Task 2

1. £30 per item
2. 266·7%

Task 3

Labour intensive as Mandy knits the items herself and does not use mechanical or automated equipment to do so.

Task 4

There are likely to be start-up costs to cover during the first few years of the business.
The business probably is not very well known to begin with – it takes time to build up the goodwill of customers.
Advertising costs are likely to be high to begin with.
The business may sell their products at a lower price to begin with to attract customers.

PAGE 101

Task 2

The bank was within its rights to do this as Lucy had another account with the same bank.

PAGE 103

Task 1

- New technology may become available meaning new equipment is introduced to the company – staff would have to be trained to use it.
- The size of the workforce may reduce, meaning staff must be trained to carry out more tasks.
- The company may be producing new products or making changes to existing products.
- The law may change, meaning that products have to be made in a different way.

Task 3

1. £9·60
2. The increasing VAT rate may put off some consumers from eating out (not just because of the extra 20 pence: they may find there is now a bigger strain on their general cost of living). The restaurant will have to recalculate their prices and reprint their menus and advertising materials.
3. a. £9·20
   b. £9·44
   c. £9·76

BUSINESS FINANCE

PAGE 104

Task 1

Grant Reynolds Upholstery
Trading, profit and loss account for year ended 31.12.10

	£	£
Sales		30 000
Less – Cost of sales		20 000
Gross profit		10 000
Expenses[4]		
Staff Wages	2000	
Rent	4000	
Electricity	1000	7000
Net profit		3000

Task 2

Grant Reynolds Upholstery Balance sheet as at 31.12.10			
		£	£
Fixed assets			
Machines			10 000
Motor vans			15 000
			25 000
Current assets			
Amount in stock		11 000	
Bank		12 000	
		23 000	
Less – current liabilities[3](owed to suppliers/creditors)		6000	
	Net current assets		17 000
	Working capital[5]		42 000
Finance			
Capital invested at start by owner			30 000
Net profit this year			12 000
			42 000

It is called a balance sheet because the working capital figure and the finance figure are equal.

PAGE 107

Task 1

One-off items:

- Alteration costs and decoration
- Physiotherapy equipment
- Seating for waiting area
- Computer and desk for admin duties
- Sign for door

Ongoing:

- Stationery (e.g. printer paper and business cards)
- Printer toner
- Consumable items like oils and creams
- Cleaning materials

Task 2

The amount her patients will be prepared to pay (e.g. average earning level).
Amount of competition in area.
The amount of profit she would like to make.
The time the treatment will take to perform.

Task 3

	Patient 1	Patient 2	Patient 3
Charge	£28·80	£30·40	£112·20
Discount	£1·44	£1·52	£5·61
Charge less discount	£27·36	£28·88	£106·59

Task 4

In business plan:

- company name and location
- type of organisation, e.g. sole trader
- main activities of business
- source of funding
- key personnel
- main competitors
- forecast profit during first year

Reasons for business plan:

- To keep the business properly on track and heading in right direction.
- To support a funding application to a bank or grant-awarding body.
- To support application to suppliers for supplies on credit.
- Information for potential investors.

PAGE 109

Task 1

Give customers less time to pay.
Negotiate a longer payment period with his suppliers.
Hold less stock.
Hold a sale to reduce the excess stock held.
Sell off any other unused assets he may have.
Reduce payments by shopping around for less expensive service providers.

Task 2

1. Target customers directly through maintaining a mailing (or email) list.
   Advertise the sale online, on local radio, in newspapers.
   Display a banner outside his premises.
2. Grant should have a policy of a deposit being paid when an order is placed, perhaps 10%, which is non-refundable. He should also have a time limit for the item to be uplifted.

Task 3

The firm could release a great deal of money by selling the prime city centre site and moving to an area where land/property is cheaper.
The new building may have lower running costs and be custom-built for modern technology.

ANSWERS

Task 4

1. It could avoid paying a large sum of money for an expensive item.
   It could sell existing assets to improve liquidity.
2. It can rely on the leasing company for maintenance and repairs.
   It can update assets as they become out-of-date.
3. The item loses value as it gets older and has had more usage.

PAGE 111

Task 1

Power 2U Energy Company: £22·75
Fast Material Supplies: £42·50

Task 2

It would depend on the percentage charged by the bank for the overdraft. They would have to compare the cost of borrowing (interest) from the bank with the penalty charge. It may be that, if the penalty charge is high, the overdraft may be the better option.

PAGE 112

Task 1

Company	Sales	Gross profit	Net profit	GP to sales percentage ratio	NP to sales percentage ratio
A	£28 000	£14 000	£7000	50%	25%
B	£36 000	£6000	£2000	16·7%	5·5%
C	£117 000	£90 000	£60 000	77%	51%

C has done the best and B has done the worst.

Task 2

Company	Total current assets	Stock	Current liabilities	Current ratio	Acid test ratio	Comments
A	£50 000	£30 000	£25 000	2 : 1	0·8 : 1	CR acceptable, ATR not acceptable
B	£36 000	£20 000	£16 000	2·25 : 1	1 : 1	Both acceptable
C	£150 000	£50 000	£70 000	2·14 : 1	1·43 : 1	Both acceptable

Task 3

Company	Total investment	Net profit	Return on capital employed
A	£60 000	£6000	10%
B	£44 000	£19 800	45%
C	£150 000	£25 000	16·7%

Company B offers the best return.

PAGE 115

Task 1

Burton Brothers: current ratio 2 : 1
Carter & Co. acid test ratio: 1 : 1.

Task 2

Company name	Position	To improve position
Afton Associates	No concern as CR is more than 2 : 1 and ATR is more than 1 : 1	
Burton Brothers	Concern with ATR as less than 1 : 1	Reduce the amount of stock held
Carter & Co	Concern with CR as less than 2 : 1	Increase amount held in bank account by giving credit customers less time to pay

Task 3

Trading, profit and loss account for year ended 20—	
Sales	£210 000
Less – cost of sales	£126 000
Gross profit	£84 000
Less expenses	£14 000
Net profit	£70 000

Gross profit to sales percentage ratio 40%
Net profit to sales percentage ratio 33·3%

PAGE 117

Task 1

Aleska is a well-qualified person who can bring her skills to the company.
As the Polish population rises in Scotland, it is good to have an employee who is a Polish speaker.

Task 2

1. Visitors from other Eurozone countries can use their own currency, which may make them more enthusiastic about coming to the UK and using UK companies.
   If the business buys stock from a Eurozone country, they don't have to change currency to do this, which reduces costs and is more convenient.
   When the company orders stock, they can be sure how much it will cost when it arrives, say, in a month's time. This gives a business stability.
   At present, some companies show prices in sterling and euros. This would no longer be necessary.
2. We have seen evidence of some Eurozone countries having problems with their economy. This problem would affect the UK significantly if the UK was in the Eurozone, causing problems for businesses.
   Software would have to be changed if we adopted the euro, which could be a big expense for businesses.
   Further expense could occur by having to train staff to use the euro.

PAGE 119

Task 1

- French: Nous espérons que vous essayerez de nos excellents produits écossais.
- German: Wir hoffen, dass Sie unsere ausgezeichnete schottischen Produkte probieren werden.
- Italian: Ci auguriamo che provare i nostri prodotti eccellenti scozzese.
- Spanish: Esperamos que probar nuestros productos escoceses excelente.

Task 2

1. Quota: A limited amount of a product that can be exported or imported from or to another country. This can protect industries in a country because it restricts competition from abroad.
2. Embargo: When an order is put in place banning imports into a country from another country. It can be used when hostility exists between two countries, possibly because one country disapproves of what the other country is doing, e.g. acting aggressively.

Task 3

Crystal and glassware
Wooden objects, e.g. ornaments
Clothing
Soft furnishings, e.g. blankets
Golfing equipment

Task 4

Many people locating in the same area can put a big strain on the infrastructure, such as housing, medical facilities and schools. Housing can become scarce, pushing house prices up.